THE RENAISSANCE OF GIRLS' EDUCATION IN ENGLAND

First published 1898
This edition published by Lector House in 2024

ISBN: 978-93-6138-723-4

Lector House LLP
Registered Office: H. No. 96, Block C, Tomar Colony,
Burari, Delhi – 110084, India
info@lectorhouse.com
www.lectorhouse.com

THE RENAISSANCE OF GIRLS' EDUCATION IN ENGLAND

ALICE ZIMMERN

2024

LECTOR HOUSE

LECTOR HOUSE LLP

THE RENAISSANCE OF GIRLS' EDUCATION IN ENGLAND

A RECORD OF FIFTY YEARS' PROGRESS

BY

ALICE ZIMMERN

(GIRTON COLLEGE, CAMBRIDGE)

AUTHOR OF 'METHODS OF EDUCATION IN AMERICA,'
'OLD TALES PROM GREECE,' ETC.

PREFACE

To all whom it may interest I dedicate this brief summary of the events which have wrought a peaceful revolution among us during the last fifty years. Among the many changes of the half-century, the great transformation in the education of women surely deserves a record. The workers have been many, the help given of various kinds, yet no event is isolated, for all are links in one chain of progress. Fifty years ago a few far-sighted men and women gave the impetus; we who harvest where they sowed may like to be reminded, in this season of retrospects, of the great debt we owe them. What has touched the lives of so many women is the concern of all, and though I shall be proud indeed if my book prove welcome to teachers, I should wish most of all to address myself to that old and long-tried friend of literature, the general reader. If he, or she, can be persuaded, to spend an hour or two, learning the past and present of the education of our girls, my purpose will have been accomplished.

To thank for favours received is a pleasant task, but the list of those who have helped me with this book would prove too long for enumeration. I desire to offer my heartiest thanks to all who have assisted me with information, criticism, or in any other way; especially to Miss Beale for valuable materials and kind hospitality, to Mrs. Bryant and Miss A. A. M. Rogers for much useful information, to Miss Mary Gurney, Miss Ella Pycroft, Miss Mary Kennedy, and Mr. W. Edwards for reading portions of the book, and to Mrs. Edwards for her sympathy and kindness during my stay in Wales. To the many headmistresses who have allowed me to visit their schools I offer most cordial thanks, and last, but not least, to the officials of the Education Library, in particular Mr. Sadler and Miss Beard, for their courtesy and helpfulness.

ALICE ZIMMERN.

September 1898.

CONTENTS

Chapter *Page*

PREFACE v

I. BEFORE 1848. 1

II. THE FIRST COLLEGES 10

III. LIGHT IN DARK PLACES 19

IV. THE HIGH SCHOOLS 26

V. ENDOWMENTS FOR GIRLS 39

VI. THE WOMEN'S COLLEGES 51

VII. ADMISSION TO UNIVERSITIES 62

VIII. BOARDING AND PRIVATE SCHOOLS 73

IX. THE TECHNICAL INSTRUCTION ACTS 83

X. STATE AID FOR GIRLS 96

XI. THE INTERMEDIATE SCHOOLS OF WALES 106

XII. 1898 115

INDEX 123

CHAPTER I

BEFORE 1848

YES, strange though it may sound, it was in truth a Renaissance—a revival of the past, and no new experiment. Or perhaps we should more fitly describe it as the realisation of an old dream, one that has been dreamed many times in the course of the ages, but has waited till the nineteenth century for its complete fulfilment. Two thousand years ago it was seen by Plato, that most practical of idealists, who maintained that it was for the best interests of the state that its men and women should be as good as possible. Therefore the education of both was a matter of public concern. In these latter days this doctrine has won acceptance, with an even wider significance, due to our democratic development. The treasures of learning are no longer the property of an exclusive few, and the privileges of class and sex are breaking down simultaneously. Education for all, boys and girls, rich and poor, is the modern demand, which no party dare now refuse to consider. We must cater not only for the 'wives of the governors,' but also for the children of the slums. All the daughters of all the households of all civilised countries are to enter into their heritage. The much-discussed 'ladder' from the elementary school to the University is becoming a fact; and its rungs are being widened, that the girls may ascend it side by side with their brothers. *La carrière ouverte aux talents,* with no distinction of class, sex, or creed, is the demand of the nineteenth century.

From Plato's Utopian 'Republic' to London of the County Council is a far cry. Between the two, this question of girls' education has many times been raised and temporarily solved. Socrates' half-jesting dictum, that women are capable of learning anything which men are willing they should know, might stand as the motto for nearly every attempt to improve female education. The instruction given to women at different epochs has varied directly with the estimation in which they were held. When they were regarded as slaves or toys it was expedient to keep them in ignorance; when they were treated honourably as equals, the best gifts of learning were not thought too good for them.

It is not our place here to dwell on the bright examples of antiquity, the Neo-Platonist women and Hypatia, the beautiful mathematician of Alexandria, but rather, turning to our own country, to see how Christianity has touched the lives of women. Here, as elsewhere, it was the Church alone that kept alive the flame of knowledge during the Middle Ages. In the seventh and eighth centuries, that 'nadir of learning,' monks and nuns alike were occupied with literary studies. They read theology and classics, copied manuscripts, and corresponded in Latin. Their activity was in accordance with their social position. 'The heads of the great religious houses were necessarily persons of importance, with privileges and great responsibilities. They had considerable wealth at their disposal, and in authority and influence they ranked among the nobles of the land, to whom they were often allied by birth.'[1] The name that naturally occurs first to our minds is that of the Abbess Hilda, 'whose counsel was sought even by kings,' and who ruled over a double monastery, which became a seminary of bishops and priests. Hers is no solitary instance. 'In Anglo-Saxon England,' writes Miss Eckenstein, 'men who attained to distinction received their training in settlements governed by women. Histories and a chronicle of unique value were inspired by and drafted under the auspices of Saxon abbesses.' And 'the curriculum of study in the nunnery was as liberal as that accepted by the monks, and embraced all available writings, whether by Christian or profane authors.' The convents were the colleges of Anglo-Saxon times. The nuns, who lived a life of seclusion and study, might be compared with the fellows; the students were the successive groups of girls who came there for education.

Among the many social changes brought about by the Norman Conquest, the most far-reaching, the introduction of feudalism, established a new centre of education, which henceforth flourished side by side with the cloister. The monks still taught the Trivium and Quadrivium—Grammar, Dialectic, Rhetoric, Music, Arithmetic, Geometry, Astronomy—though the instruction given deserved these high-sounding names little better than the so-called sciences taught in girls' schools at the beginning of our own century. The castle could offer boys a more attractive programme. The seven knightly accomplishments were to ride, sing, shoot with the bow, box, hawk, play chess, and write verses. It had something for girls as well. While the young squires gained their training by service done to their lord, the *châtelaine* would gather about her a troop of gentle maidens, who learned to weave, spin, brew, and distil, and do various kinds of needlework. They learned a little reading and writing, and in these arts were somewhat in advance of their brothers, who were trained to look on books as monkish and womanish, and not quite suited to a knight and gentleman. The *châtelaine* herself held an honourable position. In her lord's absence she must even take command of the castle, and the *damoiselles* must be prepared for their own coming responsibilities.

The thirteenth century brought a change. The political influence of the Church, which had been lessened by the Conquest, was revived by the preaching friars. They introduced a new ideal of monastic life; the spirit of devotion and asceticism drove out the old love of learning. New priories sprang up throughout England, but their aims were different. As the monasteries were more and more becoming centres of devotion, learning was being driven into the new universities, where the philosophy of the schoolmen now reigned supreme. Already some colleges with endowments for poor scholars had been founded at Oxford and Cambridge, and it was becoming the custom for the monasteries to send their most promising pupils there. Why did the nuns not follow this example? Probably the metaphysical disputations then in vogue had few attractions for them; and the presence of large numbers of men would be a sufficient reason for keeping aloof, for though the

[1] G. Hill, *Women in English Life*.

studies of both sexes might be the same, they were not pursued side by side. Whatever the cause, it is certain that while masculine learning showed an ever-growing tendency to leave the cloister, female scholarship was still closely confined to the convent. But it was degenerating for want of new life; the nunneries were a survival, not a living growth; their learning had become 'poor in substance, cramped in method, and insufficient in application.'[2] The old order was changing, but somehow the nuns failed to perceive it. In Erasmus' day, we are told, the really learned woman was to be found outside the convent walls, and he adds the significant remark that her husband approved of her studies. The wrong done to women by the dissolution was not so much the closing of the convents as the transference to men of their endowments. The most flagrant instance is the transformation of St. Radegund's nunnery at Cambridge into Jesus College. That this and other instances of spoliation were possible shows how low the status of women had sunk, and it is not strange, therefore, that a period of neglected education should have ensued.

Whatever the cause, the Reformation does not seem to have assisted the development of women. Perhaps this was partly due to the removal of the one career that had been open to them, thus forcing all, married and unmarried, into a dependent position in the household. Luther's views on women were not very elevated, and probably a good many of the Reformers shared them. It may be due to this Protestant influence that in England women profited less intellectually by the Renaissance than men, or at any rate in far smaller numbers. Thanks to the new grammar schools, learning was being made accessible to boys of all classes. When Sir Thomas More's dream was realised, and the middle classes, from the squire to the petty tradesman, were brought into contact with ancient literature, the daughters were not as well provided as the sons. Some authorities are of opinion that the original foundations were meant for both sexes alike, but if so, very few girls of the middle class profited by their advantages, though some sort of education evidently came to all. Among the upper classes large numbers of women were carried away by the enthusiasm of the Renaissance, and learned to read Latin and Greek. The sixteenth century has always been celebrated for its learned ladies, as witness Wotton's oft quoted remark thereon and his comment: 'One would think by the effects that it was a proper way of educating them, since there are no accounts in history of so many great women in any age as are to be found between the years 1500 and 1600.' Queen Elizabeth and Lady Jane Grey are sometimes called exceptions, but this is clearly an error. Learning was an expensive luxury for women, since it involved the services of a private tutor, but it had fashion and opinion on its side. To be learned was accounted a privilege, which called for neither arrogant boasting nor blushing concealment. Those who did study, would naturally turn to the best their age could offer them, *i.e.* the new editions of the classics and the fashionable modern literature. They set the fashion too as well as followed it. The success of *Euphues* was established by its lady readers, and in the domain of polite literature it was generally acknowledged that they created the standard. When Lyly wrote 'Euphues had rather lie shut in a lady's casket than open in a scholar's study,' he knew well enough that it was not the ladies who would neglect his book. He confessed as much in its dedication to the 'Ladies and Gentlewomen of

[2] L. Eckenstein, *Women under Monasticism.*

England.' Nor was there anything new in this. The lady sat in her bower to read Sidney's *Arcadia* as in olden times she had listened in the hall to the lay of the minstrel. It was still her part to assign the prize of romance as of valour. The leisure which made the enjoyment of tale and song possible was essentially the lot of the rich and noble lady, who neither toiled nor span, but did a more useful work as guardian of art and literature. The amazing discovery that 'Books are a part of man's prerogative'[3] had not yet been made; there is certainly not a hint of it in Shakespeare. Nor could such a doctrine possibly originate under a queen, who, whatever her faults, cultivated learning herself and honoured it in others. Our thoughts linger lovingly over that noblest age of English story, when romanticism and classicism joined their glories for a brief space; when the courtier was both knight and scholar, and the noble dame's epitaph praised her as 'wise and fair and good.' Seen through the haze of the past, its splendours stand out in even greater dimension, while all that was small and weak is obscured to dimness. The very age that followed served as a foil to throw into yet brighter relief 'the spacious days of great Elizabeth.'

It is significant of the rapid degeneration that ensued, that though between the accession of Henry VIII. and the death of James I., 353 grammar schools were founded in England, not one was added to the number after 1625. The seventeenth century was a gloomy period for England. If Elizabeth had given her country peace and glory, the Stuarts were not long in reversing the position. Disastrous civil wars, political and theological quarrels, absorbed the best energies of the nation. The Cavaliers were too frivolous, the Roundheads too grimly earnest to spare much leisure for learning. In times of war and national peril woman's influence is apt to wane, and such power as they had at the Stuart court was not of the kind to encourage intellectual pursuits. When a scholar was hardly accounted a gentleman, a lady might be pardoned for neglecting her intellectual charms. It became the fashion among men to decry female students, to bid them put away their books and learn to wash and cook instead. 'I like not a female poetess at any hand,' says one of these self-appointed critics. This attitude was characteristic of the decline of chivalry and the degradation of woman's position. 'There is not so much as a Don Quixote of the quill left,' writes Mary Astell in 1694, 'to succour the distressed damsels.' The age of courtesy being over, women must help themselves, and she takes up the cudgels for her sex. 'A man ought no more to value himself on being wiser than a woman,' she remarks pertinently, 'if he owes his advantage to a better education and greater means of information, than he ought to boast of courage for beating a man when his hands were bound.'[4] Hers is the old thesis, that women are quite capable of learning if only men will not put hindrances in their way. Even so the girls' curriculum of her day does not seem to have been as meagre as is often assumed. She tells us that when the boys go to grammar schools the girls are sent 'to boarding-schools or other places to learn needlework, dancing, singing, music, drawing, painting, and other accomplishments ... and French, which is now very fashionable.' This description which would almost have served at the beginning of our own century, is not as gloomy as Defoe's, written at about the same time. Girls,

[3] Sir Th. Overbury.

[4] Mary Astell. *An Essay in Defence of the Female Sex.*

he tells us, learned 'to stitch and sew and make baubles. They are taught to read indeed, and perhaps to write their names or so, and this is the height of a woman's education.'[5] Both agree in condemning its narrowness. Defoe cannot believe that 'God Almighty ever made them such glorious creatures, and furnished them with such charms, so agreeable and delightful to mankind, with souls capable of the same accomplishment with men, and all to be only stewards of our houses, cooks, and slaves.' Mary Astell maintains that 'according to the rate that young women are educated, according to the way their time is spent, they are destined to folly and impertinence, to say no worse.' She protests, as Mrs. Makins had done before her,[6] against the new fashion of ignorant women, and implores her sisters to help bring back the good old times, and take a lesson from the ladies of the previous century. Both Defoe and Mary Astell recommend the same project, the establishment of women's colleges, thus anticipating our own times by more than a century and a half. Defoe's colleges would have been superior boarding-schools, one in every county and about ten for the city of London; Mary Astell's plan was to combine religious and intellectual aims. She contemplated 'a seminary to stock the kingdom with pious and prudent ladies, whose good example, it is to be hoped, will so influence the rest of their sex, that women may no longer pass for those little, useless, and impertinent animals which the ill conduct of too many has caused them to be mistaken for.'[7] But it must also try to 'expel that cloud of ignorance which custom has involved us in, to furnish our minds with a stock of solid and useful knowledge, that the souls of women may no longer be the only unadorned and neglected things.' Nothing came of either project; they belong to the domain of unfulfilled dreams.

The new century brought little improvement. Anne was not of a sufficiently independent character to influence greatly the lives and pursuits of her subjects. As was natural in the reign of a Queen, the position and dignity of women were somewhat raised; and in that 'Augustan age' there was one class of literature specially addressed to the ladies, the newly invented essay. Addison really wanted to elevate their position and social influence, but his success was literary rather than moral. If we may trust the novelists of the last century, public morality was never at a lower ebb. The men of that day worshipped idleness, and it was not surprising that they did not care to see their wives and mistresses at work. Show was the aim throughout, and the 'accomplishment' reigned supreme. The second half of the century witnessed a great increase in the boarding-school system. Hitherto it had been confined to the fashionable world; now tradesmen and farmers who had made some money began to emulate their 'betters.' Imitations of the fashionable schools sprang up everywhere. 'We have,' says the heroine of General Burgoyne's play, *The Heiress*, "Young ladies boarded and educated" upon blue boards in gold letters in every village; with a strolling player for a dancing-master, and a deserter from Dunkirk to teach the French language.'

The eighteenth century, too, had its distinguished women; indeed, the Blue-Stocking Club, so called, it seems, from the dress of one of its masculine *habi-*

[5] Defoe. *Essay on Projects.*

[6] Mrs. Makins. *An Essay to Revive the Ancient Education of Gentlewomen*, 1673.

[7] Mary Astell. *A Serious Proposal.*

tués, is regarded as the representative group of learned ladies. But Mrs. Montagu, Mrs. Chapone, and Hannah More were exceptions, and themselves only too conscious of their opposition to the rest of their sex. There was a touch of the *précieuse* about some of them which exposed them to a good deal of cheap satire, and they were keenly alive to the antagonism with which the other sex regarded them. Mrs. Chapone even advises her niece to avoid the study of classics and science, for fear of 'exciting envy in one sex and jealousy in the other.' Lady Mary Wortley Montagu complains bitterly that 'there is hardly a creature in the world more despicable and more liable to universal ridicule than that of a learned woman,' while 'folly is reckoned so much our proper sphere, we are sooner pardoned any excesses of that than the least pretensions to reading and good sense.'

Some of these last century women were practical reformers, who realised the pernicious results of this false opinion about their sex. Among these was Hannah More, who entered a most earnest protest against the excessive accomplishment craze. The lower middle class were emulating the upper in their endeavour to make their daughters 'accomplished young ladies,' while they quite forgot that 'the profession of ladies to which the best of their education should be turned is that of daughters, wives, mothers, and mistresses of families.'[8] She even ventured to fly in the face of public opinion by asserting that 'a young lady may excel in speaking French and Italian, may repeat a few passages from a volume of extracts, play like a professor, and sing like a siren,' and yet be very badly educated, if her mind remains untrained. 'The kind of knowledge that they commonly do acquire is easily attained,' they learn everything in a superficial question-and-answer way, or through abridgments, beauties, and compendiums, instead of reading books that require thought and attention. As we read her *Strictures on Female Education* we rub our eyes and look at the date once more. Is this, indeed, Hannah More writing a hundred years ago, or have we stumbled upon a stray extract from Mr. Bryce's report to the Schools' Inquiry Commission in 1867? 'She should pursue every kind of study which will teach her to elicit truth, which will lead her to be intent upon realities; will give precision to her ideas; will make an exact mind.' She quotes Dr. Johnson's opinion that 'a woman cannot have too much arithmetic.' Had the worthy doctor a prevision of a High School time-table?

Hannah More's influence does not seem to have been very lasting. Her contemptuous remark, that we might as well talk about the rights of children as the rights of women, shows that she had not much real grasp of the educational problem. Both should, in her opinion, be relegated to their proper subordinate places. She was right in despising the frivolity of her day, and condemning the constant round of pleasure in which fashionable women spent their lives, but she was almost too severe to be helpful. Far more valuable was Miss Edgeworth's work, which was constructive as well as critical. Her educational romances, in which she contrasts the good and bad governess, the sensible and frivolous girl, are thoroughly readable even at the present day, and must have proved useful to many readers who lighted unawares on the powder in the jam. *Practical Education*, written in conjunction with her father, throws valuable light on contemporary conditions,

[8] Hannah More. *Strictures on Female Education.*

and advances theories that are still worthy of our notice. The 'practical toy shop,' provided with all manner of carpenter's tools, with wood properly prepared for the young workman, and with screws, nails, glue, emery-paper, etc., is still to seek; her remarks on the two schools, the one teaching 'by dint of reiterated pain and terror,' the other 'with the help of counters and coaxing and gingerbread,' are not altogether out of date. Nor have we yet learned to pay a good governess £300 a year, on the ground that her working days are few, and she ought to lay by for a comfortable old age. Her severest strictures, like Hannah More's, are reserved for 'female accomplishments.' Their chief use is that 'they are supposed to increase a young lady's chance of a prize in the matrimonial lottery.' Hence, when the end is achieved, they are thrown aside. 'As soon as a young lady is married, does she not frequently discover that she really has no leisure to cultivate talents which take up so much time?' Nor is it quite certain that they are as efficacious as is generally supposed. The market is becoming overstocked, for 'every young lady, and every young woman is now a young lady, has some pretension to accomplishments. She draws a little; or she plays a little; or she speaks French a little.' Accomplishments are becoming so general 'that they cannot be considered as the distinguishing characteristics of even a gentlewoman's education.' Since they are no longer 'exclusive,' she hopes they may be cast aside for something better. Her indictment against the female education of her day is that 'sentiment and ridicule have conspired to represent reason, knowledge, and science as unsuitable and dangerous to women; yet, at the same time, wit and superficial acquirements in literature have been the object of admiration in society; so that this dangerous inference has been drawn, almost without our perceiving its fallacy, that superficial knowledge is more desirable in women than accurate knowledge.' It is interesting to find this complaint repeated in 1826 by an anonymous writer,[9] who maintains the old dictum that 'females are not behind males in capacity, and excel them in diligence and docility,' but they are handicapped by 'an education of mere externals and of show.' There is a want of stamina in girls' education, and as for their school-books, they are mere combinations of words used as 'substitutes or apologies for ideas.'

Maria Edgeworth's influence should have been considerable, but turning from her works to her contemporaries and immediate successors, it seems doubtful whether they even understood her. Her stories, whose most useful lessons were addressed to parents, were turned into children's books; and the demand for a more solid education simply led to an increase of the memory and book-work in schools. In spite of her strictures on the uselessness of a knowledge of isolated facts, and the attempts of Mrs. Barbauld and others to supply something better, the catechism system continued to grow and flourish. Large amounts of memory work were added to the piano and drawing, which still held their own, and the results were not merely negative as regards intellectual value, but positive in their injurious effects on health. Miss Frances Power Cobbe in her description of the fashionable boarding-school to which she was sent in 1836, speaks of the pages of prose the girls were expected to learn by heart, amid the din of constant practising. 'Not that which was good in itself or useful to the community, or even that which would be delightful to ourselves, but that which would make us admired in soci-

[9] *The Complete Governess.* A Course of Mental Instruction for Ladies.

ety was the *raison-d'être* of each requirement. Everything was taught in the inverse ratio of its true importance. At the bottom of the scale were Morals and Religion, and at the top were Music and Dancing, miserably poor music too, of the Italian school then in vogue, and generally performed in a showy and tasteless manner on harp or piano.'[10] Miss Cobbe thinks this education far worse than that received by her mother in 1790, when much less was attempted, and there was no 'packing the brains of girls with facts.' Besides 'grammar and geography, and a very fair share of history' (ancient from Rollin, and sacred from Mrs. Trimmer), they 'learned to speak and read French with a very good accent, and to play the harpsichord with taste.' Clearly things were on the downward course, and in the first half of this century the education of both sexes was in some respects in a worse condition in England than at any time before or since. Mere ignorance would have been comparatively harmless, but there never was a time when educational theories were more fashionable or more perverse. Miss Catherine Sinclair, who wrote in the forties and fifties, lifted up her voice, in *Modern Accomplishments*, against the system of cram and display then prevailing. 'Lady Howard's utmost ingenuity was exercised in devising plans of study for her daughter, each of which required to be tried under the dynasty of a different governess, so that by the time Matilda Howard attained the age of sixteen, she had been successively taught by eight, all of whom were instructed in the last method that had been invented for making young ladies accomplished on the newest pattern.' All these governesses were foreign, according to the fashion of the day; at last an English lady of Edgworthian type was discovered, who trained the mind instead of overloading the memory, and all ended happily. Precocity and display were what parents demanded, and schools and governesses contrived to supply the requirements. Miss Sinclair's accounts of premature death and lifelong ill-health may have been overdrawn, but doubtless she put her finger on the weak spot when she wrote: 'Nothing is popular now that requires thought in young people, who are constantly devouring books, but never digesting them, and are allowed no time to think.'

The better the school, in the acceptation of that day, the worse probably the result; and those girls whose parents could not afford the expensive governess or the 'finishing-school,' often had the best of it, so long as they were not sent to one of the cheap and inefficient imitations. By a curious irony the one attempt made early in the century to give a good education at a small expense, was that which through Charlotte Brontë's genius has been held up to everlasting contumely. The Clergy Daughters' School at Cowen Bridge undertook, for the small sum of £14 a year, to clothe, feed, lodge, and educate the daughters of clergymen. In 1825, the year when Charlotte Brontë was there, the Rev. W. Carus Wilson (too well known as Mr. Brocklehurst), appealing for additional funds, stated that an annual income of £250, together with the fees, would be sufficient to meet current expenses. A comparison of this modest demand with the sums raised in our own day for women's colleges, helps us to realise the revolution that has taken place in public opinion. Even so most of the subscribers seem to have been Mr. Wilson's relations, and it was only as a charity for the poor clergy, with a side-thought of getting better governesses at low terms, that it awakened any interest at all. Still it was

[10] *Autobiography of Frances Power Cobbe.*

considered a remarkable achievement. In 1833, Mr. Venn Elliott, who had visited the school in its new premises at Casterton, and been present at the consecration of the church built in its neighbourhood, wrote: 'I would rather have built this school and church than Blenheim and Burleigh. So Dr. Watts said he would rather have written Baxter's *Call to the Unconverted* than Milton's *Paradise Lost*.' The result of this visit was the foundation of St. Mary's Hall at Brighton. It still exists, and gives a really first-class education at a low fee. Other schools were founded in imitation; and in spite of the sordid economy of those early days, and the suffering it entailed on the weakly, they deserve full recognition as almost the only institutions which attempted in the early part of the century to provide a good and cheap education for girls. The tradition of sound study survived, and in 1867 the Casterton institution came in for a word of praise from the Royal Commissioners, amid their almost universal condemnation of existing girls' schools.

The benefits which a woman's reign always confers on women have been experienced to the full during the long and peaceful reign of our present Queen. The interest taken by her and the Prince Consort in arts and letters, and in the general improvement of the people, set an example that was readily followed. Ladies of the upper and middle classes began to take a keener interest in the lives of the poor, and in dealing with the problems they thus encountered were often brought to realise their own want of education. There was a stir and a movement towards something better. The views of men were gradually changing, as the ideal of womanhood set by a purer Court became more elevated. Sixty years of a woman's wise and beneficent rule have done much to restore the glories of Elizabeth's day. Like the revival of letters, which communicated to the whole world the learning which had once belonged to one small people, this other renaissance brought knowledge, not only to the convent pupil and the lady of leisure, but to all the daughters of the nation. This widening has helped to fix the roots more firmly, and we may hope and believe that the gains of this century are not to be lost, but, enriched by all the wealth of the future, to continue for many a generation to come.

CHAPTER II

THE FIRST COLLEGES

The revival of women's education in England has now a record of fifty years behind it. On the 1st of May this year Queen's College in Harley Street celebrated its Jubilee with manifold rejoicings, a celebration in which all Englishwomen may claim the right to join. Though Girton and Holloway and other newer institutions have arisen since to throw the glories of Queen's into the shade, none can deprive it of its proud title—the first women's college in England.

An occasion of this kind provokes reminiscence and the drawing of contrasts between 1848 and 1898; while the question that naturally occurs to us is: How did it all begin? Many answers have been suggested. Some have pressed the significance of 1848 as the year of Revolution, and hinted that the women's share in revolt was an attempt to throw off the shackles of ignorance. This may not be altogether fanciful. Such social upheavals symbolise the workings of intellectual forces, nor can we doubt that the attempt to win for women privileges from which they had hitherto been jealously excluded is a part of the democratic demand for universal equal opportunity.

Along with the general ferment of ideas and the cry for reform must be counted the growing influence on the lives of the upper classes exercised by the Queen and Prince Consort. Following the lead of the Court the ideals of the nation were changing. A more serious view of life and its responsibilities was developing, and the time seemed a propitious one for organised effort. But though various schemes had been discussed, the immediate impetus to action was an actual and crying need. In those days girls of the upper classes were, for the most part, educated at home by governesses, usually foreigners, because Englishwomen, though glad enough to obtain such posts, when suddenly thrown upon the world by the death of a parent or other untoward circumstance, were seldom properly qualified to fill them. Some of course there were who, by foreign travel or private study, had reached a fair standard of attainment; but how distinguish these from the herd, when they lacked even the teacher's diploma with which their Swiss or German rivals were equipped? In this dilemma the Governesses' Benevolent Institution came to the rescue.

This Institution had been founded in 1843 with a threefold aim:—(1) To afford temporary relief in cases of great suffering, (2) To cultivate provident habits in those who could afford to save; (3) To raise annuities for those past work. This programme seemed to distinguish governesses as a class specially in need of pity and relief. To attempt to help them by increasing their competency, and thus indirectly their wage-earning capacity, was a bold new departure. The first proposal was to hold examinations for a teacher's diploma, but it soon appeared that an attempt to examine the untaught was a useless inversion of the natural order. To make the undertaking really helpful it became necessary to institute a system of classes. This scheme was first discussed in 1846, and a sum of money collected by Miss Murray, one of the Queen's Maids of Honour, handed over to the Institution for this purpose. In 1847 the first certificates were conferred, and arrangements made for opening classes. Here some of the most distinguished professors of King's College stepped in with help. Among them were Maurice, Trench, and Kingsley, and others no less noted. It was a new and astounding departure for men of their standing to be willing to lecture to women. They began with evening classes, but soon added others in the day for ladies of no special occupation. This led to the taking of 67 Harley Street, for the purpose of holding classes in 'all branches of female learning,' and permission was received to name the new institution Queen's College.

On March 29, 1848, Professor F. D. Maurice, who has been called the 'parent and founder of the College,' delivered an inaugural address on 'Queen's College, London, its objects and methods.' After apologising for the word 'college' as somewhat too ambitious for the project in hand, he thought well to answer in advance the objections of those who might use Pope's hackneyed line about 'a little learning' as a means of discrediting the new classes. Even he did not anticipate very deep draughts from the spring of knowledge. 'We are aware that our pupils are not likely to advance far in mathematics, but we believe that if they learn really what they do learn, they will not have got what is dangerous but what is safe.... I cannot conceive that a young lady can feel her mind in a more dangerous state than it was, because she has gained a truer glimpse into the conditions under which the world in which it has pleased God to place her actually exists.'

Each of the first courses was preceded by a preliminary lecture, in which the professor introduced, and almost apologised for his subject. Latin was to win toleration as 'one road, and perhaps the shortest, to a thorough study of English'; in each case it was shown that the evils anticipated from that particular subject were fanciful. These explanations strike us quaintly now; it is hard to realise how great was the terror of learned ladies which in those days it was fashionable to assume.

Still, in spite of prejudice, the College flourished. There were no less than two hundred entries the first term. In 1853 it had grown sufficiently independent to stand on its own feet, and breaking away from the parent institution, it was incorporated by Royal Charter. Its objects were declared to be the general education of ladies, and the granting of certificates of knowledge. Professor Maurice became Chairman of Committee and Principal; and Queen's, which loves its old traditions, has continued the practice of appointing a male Principal, therein differing from every other women's college in the United Kingdom. It feels so keenly the debt it owes its founders, that it cherishes the idea—mistaken surely—that it can best do them honour by maintaining the college such as it was in their day. Thus the fate of many a pioneer has overtaken Queen's. The vanguard have become the laggards, and useful and admirable as is its work, it has been outstripped by younger institutions, and no longer stands in the forefront of the battle. This is the common fate; it is easier to improve than to originate, but the debt of gratitude we all owe to Queen's is none the less because so many others have harvested where she sowed.

Since Queen's takes pride in its conservatism and adherence to its original methods, the latest calendar gives a very fair idea of its work even in early days. It states that 'the College provides for the higher education of women, in the first place by a liberal school training, and, subsequently, by a four years' course of College education. The College education leads to the grade of Associate ... and after a further course of study to the higher grade of Fellow of the College.' The school was not part of the original scheme, but became necessary when the first generation of students, thoughtful women who had already been trying to improve themselves, and eagerly welcomed the advantages then for the first time offered them, gave way to a younger generation. Among the applicants for admission were mere schoolgirls, and instead of turning them away to seek inefficient preparation elsewhere, it was resolved to start a preparatory department for their benefit. This developed into a small school for girls under fourteen, the age at which pupils are admitted into the College. Here the students belong to two categories: those who follow a prescribed course laid down by the authorities, and those who enter for single classes, and arrange their work themselves. The former class are known as 'compounders,' and pay a composition fee of £8 to £10 per term. They must attend eighteen hours a week of regular class teaching. The regulations fix the subjects for twelve hours; parents or guardians for the other six. The prescribed work includes—(*a*) two languages: English, two hours, and French, German, Latin, or Greek, two hours; (*b*) two sciences: Mathematics and Arithmetic, four hours; Geography, one hour, Natural Philosophy, one hour, when exemption is granted in Mathematics; (*c*) English History, one hour, Ancient or Modern History, one hour; (*d*) Holy Scripture, one hour.

Candidates for the Fellowship must have passed the examination for the Associateship at least one academical year previously to entering for the Fellowship examination. For this, one principal subject of study must be chosen, with not fewer than two additional subjects. Since only three students had, in 1897, concluded this additional course, the Associateship may be regarded as the ordinary goal of Queen's College students. The course for this is excellent, doubtless, for girls from fourteen to eighteen; but studies of so miscellaneous a character, leading to a 'grade' which can be attained at the age of eighteen, belong properly to the domain of school work. Queen's differs, however, in its organisation from the upper department of a modern High School. Most of the teaching is given in the form of lectures. This lecture-system marks a distinct stage in the progress of girls' education. In the schools of the early part of the century the various 'professors' who came to lecture occupied an important place in the prospectus. They ranged freely over the sciences in a manner that amused and interested their hearers, without making any undue demand upon their intelligence or powers of thought. Hence, the lecture-system seems to have established itself as a first step towards attracting female pupils to the higher branches of knowledge. The High Schools, too, were to pass through that stage, and emerge from it. Queen's still keeps up the tradition of lectures, and as its discipline and general arrangements differ from those of a school, without resembling those of a college, it must be regarded as an institution apart, self-contained, and unconnected. As such it is of the greatest value in supplementing the home-teaching of girls, or undertaking the complete education of those who do not desire to enter the University, or take up any distinct profession. These would probably get a better practical preparation at a good high school. Still the others are likely to remain the majority, and there will always be an important function for an institution that supplies good teaching without any compulsion to enter for outside examination. Such, at any rate, is the view of the Council, who have commemorated their Jubilee by a renewal of the lease, and the general improvement and partial reconstruction of the premises. In its old home, with unbroken traditions, gathering in the children and grandchildren of its earliest students, it is continuing the work with which, fifty years ago, it inaugurated the revival of women's education.

Although Queen's was the first college actually opened, other similar schemes were being projected at the same time. The foundation in 1826 of University College had given an impetus to advanced studies in London, and as a perfectly undenominational institution it served as the model for Bedford Ladies' College. The foundress and benefactor of Bedford was Mrs. Reid. Her wish to help girls took effect in 1847 in the establishment of classes at her own house. Two years later she took a house in Bedford Square and gave £1500 towards the initial expenses. Mrs. Reid and her friends were ambitious. They meant to found a real place of higher education for women, and in doing so they did not hesitate to break with the past. Mrs. Reid felt convinced that women could best understand the needs of girls, and though a committee consisting chiefly of men might at that time have included more distinguished names, she probably kept in mind the time to come when the college would be able to invite its own old pupils on to its committee. The co-operation of ladies was in the first instance secured by the institution of lady-visitors, to be present in turn at lectures—a plan at that time considered indispensable, and adopted also at Queen's. It was arranged that the College Board should include the forty lady-visitors and six gentlemen. This Board annually appointed the Council of Management, and the Council elected the professors and all the officers of the college. This plan seemed to answer, and the college, which was fortunate enough to secure the services of such able men as De Morgan, F. W. Newman, and Dr. Carpenter, entered on a successful career. After a while pupils came in from a distance. Provision had to be made for these, and in 1861 a second house was taken and the upper floors adapted as a residence, while the lower ones were used for class-rooms. For a few years Bedford too had to maintain a school, but this was not part of the promoters' scheme, and they hailed the first signs of improved school teaching as a pretext for closing it. This happened in 1868, at a time when circumstances made a complete reorganisation of the college necessary with a distinct declaration of policy.

The change had been hastened by the death of Mrs. Reid. She left a considerable part of her fortune in the charge of three trustees, Miss Bostock, Miss J. Martineau, and Miss E. E. Smith, to be utilised for 'purposes of higher education.'

This seemed a suitable moment to seek incorporation, and in 1869 Bedford College received its charter. Its objects were thus described:

'1. To continue with an improved constitution the College for women which has been carried on since 1849 in Bedford Square, London, and has been known since the year 1860 as Bedford College.

'2. To provide thereby a liberal education for women, such education not to extend beyond secular subjects.'

Henceforth the management was vested in members of the college, with a Council elected from the number and a President, to be called the Visitor. This office has been held successively by Erasmus Darwin, Mark Pattison, and Miss Anna Swanwick.

Bedford, like Queen's, was happy in its founders, but to none does it owe more than to Miss Bostock. After Mrs. Reid's death she took over the care of the college as a sacred trust, devoting to it the greater part of her time, and helping it with money and good counsel. Happily she lived to see the fruit of her labours, and to know that Bedford College had won an assured position through its connection with the London University.

Its beginnings, like that of most women's institutions, had to be tentative. The first lectures probably had a more popular character than those now given; and since they aimed rather at general culture than a systematic course of study, Literature, History, and Language would draw the largest audiences. But from the very first Latin, Science, and Mathematics were taught, and the college remembers with due pride that George Eliot was a member of its earliest Latin class. At any rate the promoters were quite sure of their aims. The daring words, 'a liberal education for women,' had been uttered without extenuation or apology. But in those days Bedford College stood alone, with no academic body to test its work and direct its curriculum. Nor was public opinion yet fully ripe for a real University education for women. Bedford had to wait another ten years before the opening of the London degrees came to fix its position and define its studies. They were not wasted years. The college was giving numbers of intelligent and eager girls their first insight into real knowledge, and teaching them to be dissatisfied with narrow, cramping instruction. Many of them have gone out into the world to hand on the impulse and inspiration gained here, and help to influence that public opinion which alone has made admission to the Universities possible. In 1874 the college was helped by a move to better premises. When in 1879 London opened its degrees to women, the opportunity of Bedford had come, and it was ready to use it. From this date onward its history belongs to that of Women's University Education.

These two earliest colleges may be regarded as not only pioneers but also parent institutions. They drew within the sphere of their influence many of those women who were to train up the next generation. Among the earliest pupils of the Queen's College evening classes was Miss Buss, who was already teaching in her mother's private school, and was destined to found the first public school for girls. She was one of the first to win the governess diploma. Another was Miss Dorothea Beale, so well known for her work at Cheltenham. She remained at Queen's from

1849 to 1856, first teaching Mathematics, then Latin, and afterwards in charge of the school. In 1858 she became Principal of the Cheltenham Ladies' College, which had already been at work for five years.

The Cheltenham College differed in its original idea from Queen's and Bedford. Both these had been founded with the purpose of giving women such advanced education as they were at that time capable of receiving, and had gradually been compelled by the exigencies of the case to provide for girls as well. Cheltenham, though called a college in imitation of the boys' college in that town and some other public schools, really aimed in the first instance at providing for girls similar educational advantages to those which their brothers enjoyed in the same town. As King's College had suggested Queen's, the boys' college at Cheltenham suggested the girls'. Twelve years elapsed between the foundation of the two; and Queen's and Bedford were already pointing the way when a small committee of enthusiasts met at the house of Mr. Bellairs, one of H.M. Inspectors, and drew up a prospectus, inviting the public to take shares in the new undertaking. A day-school was all that was at first contemplated, and the subjects to be taught there were described as Holy Scripture and the Liturgy, history, geography, grammar, arithmetic, French, music, drawing, needlework. German, Italian, and dancing to be extras. The proposal found favour. Shares to the amount of about £2000 were taken up, a house hired, and the new venture started with good auspices, 88 pupils entering the first term, and the numbers soon going up to 120. It is not quite easy to understand why this prosperous beginning was not followed up. After a while the numbers went down, and the college seemed to be losing favour. Probably it was ahead of local public opinion, not yet abreast of North London, where Miss Buss was already successfully at work. The first years were times of struggle, and even the appointment of Miss Beale in 1858 did not at once turn the scale. After forty years of successful work in the college, Miss Beale can enjoy the pleasure of contrasting then and now. Some of her reminiscences throw a curious light on public opinion in the early fifties. The curriculum, unpretentious as it seems, proved too advanced. Parents objected to the thoroughness of the teaching, and the time given to arithmetic and similar subjects. Some disliked the annual examination, which was held to be unfeminine, and the difficulty of obtaining good teachers was almost insuperable. In regard to these Miss Beale suffered through being ahead of her times. She desired especially two things: that the teachers should be women, for, to quote her own words, 'we think it essential to the right moral training of girls that the whole internal discipline and much of the moral training should be in the hands of ladies'; and that they should be to some extent specialists, the only way to abolish the textbook cram and unintelligent memory work then in vogue in girls' schools. How she set out again and again to seek for teachers, and how many a time she was disappointed, she has herself recorded in her history of the college. Her efforts show how hard it was to found a school before the reformation of the higher education had given the necessary impetus from above. It was a case of making bricks without straw.

Perhaps the practical difficulties in the way of finance were really the most hampering, for the founders had too little experience of these matters; and a Mr.

Brancker, who as treasurer, by readjusting the whole system of fees, put the College on a sound financial basis, may almost count as its second founder.

In 1863, five years after Miss Beale took office, some Oxford examiners were invited to inspect and report on the school. This was a new departure; it meant an acknowledgment of the connection which should exist between girls' schools and the Universities. A small thing in itself, but typical of the many changes that the next five-and-twenty years were to bring.

From this time onward the College was brought into close connection with every educational reform in England; and its history, like that of the North London Collegiate, presents in miniature the various changes of this busy quarter of a century. In 1863 an informal examination was held for girls in the papers of the Cambridge Local Examination. This was the beginning of a new departure, and from that time forth preparation for one or other of the local University examinations formed part of the work of both schools. In 1866, Miss Beale and Miss Buss were called upon to give evidence before the Royal Commission, and the plan of these two schools was thus brought before the notice of the general public. The interest that resulted in all questions concerning the education of girls reacted on these first schools. For Miss Buss it won an endowment, for Cheltenham that recognition which means success. It became possible to raise the standard and enlarge the curriculum. Mathematics, Science, Latin and Greek, were added to the prospectus. Applications from pupils outside the town necessitated the opening of a boarding-house in 1864. The College was fast outgrowing its first home; then came a fresh obstacle to overcome. Building had become essential, but prejudice stood in the way. Although good premises and beautiful surroundings have long been regarded as essential for boys' schools and colleges and a really important factor in the training given there, the prejudice that any makeshift was good enough for girls has died hard, if indeed it can even now be called dead. Miss Beale naturally desired to see the now flourishing College in adequate and beautiful buildings. This seemed to some of the governors too daring a departure. However, after many struggles and defeats, the party of progress carried the day. The new premises, the nucleus of the present beautiful College buildings, were opened in 1873. Of course they had the effect of attracting additional numbers; and when three years later, further extension became necessary, it appeared that the College had not merely outgrown its premises, but also its constitution. The time had come to put it on a more lasting basis. At a meeting of shareholders it was decided to renounce all claim on a profit, and accept instead a right of nomination on each share, as is done at several boys' proprietary schools. The whole income became available for the payment of teachers, the maintenance and improvement of the buildings, school furniture and apparatus. The government was placed in the hands of a council of twenty-four persons, six being representative members chosen by the Bishop of the Diocese, the Universities of Oxford, Cambridge, and London, the Lady Principal and the staff of teachers, while the remaining eighteen were elected by the shareholders. The inclusion of women on this body has proved specially beneficial to the College.

By this time there were 500 girls in the school, and ten licensed boarding-houses. Many internal changes had taken place, corresponding to the changes in the world without. The Cambridge Local Examinations had proved helpful in the early days, and the establishment in 1868 of the Cambridge Higher Local supplied a definite aim for the work of the senior classes. It has always been popular at Cheltenham, and over 500 girls have passed it from the College. Another impetus was given to work by the institution of the special women's examination of the University of London; during the nine years of its existence, one-third of the successful candidates came from Cheltenham. But it was the formal opening of the London degrees that led to the present complete organisation of the College with its system of departments, leading respectively to the Oxford Senior, Cambridge Higher, and London University Examinations. By this time Girton, Newnham, and other women's colleges had come into existence. Cheltenham could send its pupils to continue their studies at the older Universities, and the specialist teachers, for whom Miss Beale had sighed in vain in the early days, were now forthcoming. Fashion too was beginning to smile on those more serious studies which the College had so long pursued in the face of prejudice. The time of struggle was over. Cheltenham was no longer in advance of the tide, but moving harmoniously with it, giving help and receiving it.

Cheltenham College, as it now exists, has certain peculiarities which distinguish it from most of the girls' schools of the present day. Firstly, it does not receive all comers, but is distinctly intended for the 'daughters of gentlemen,' and references in regard to social standing are required before admission. Secondly, it combines the functions of a day and boarding-school, by a system of boarding-houses which belong to the Council, and are under the general control and supervision of the Principal. Thirdly, it is not one large school, but a system of departments under separate heads, all under the direction of the Principal. Division I. is under Miss Beale herself. The work is directed towards: (1) the London Degrees; (2) the Cambridge Higher Local; (3) the Oxford Senior and Higher Local Examinations. This division is the College proper, and is organised to some extent on college lines. Division II. has about 200 pupils between twelve and sixteen. Division III., the juvenile department, has about 70 pupils between seven and twelve. Below this comes the Kindergarten. By-students may attend single courses of lectures as at Queen's and Bedford.

Cheltenham College is thus enabled from its own resources to take a child straight from the nursery, and after many years send her forth as a full-fledged graduate of London University. It is neither to be expected nor desired that many girls should thus receive the whole of their education under one roof, but while some attend one department and some another, the College does in itself comprise the three stages of education: primary, secondary, higher. It has gone even further, for it takes an important part in the work of training teachers, which has been so largely developed of late years. The training department has three distinct divisions, in which teachers are prepared for Kindergarten, Secondary, and Public Elementary Schools. The 'Hall of Residence,' which is growing so much in favour now, is also represented at Cheltenham by St. Hilda's, a residential college for students over eighteen, and in particular the twenty foundationers who are intending teachers and are received at reduced fees. Finally, the Old Girls' Guild with its eleven hundred members all over the world, its College Settlement in the East End of London, and its biennial meetings at Cheltenham, keeps the College in constant touch with the work, social, philanthropic, and professional, that is being done by women at the present day.

The Cheltenham College has become a little world of itself. It presents in miniature each of the developments in women's education which has taken place in the last fifty years. The dignity of its beautiful buildings, the ideals which take visible form in the statues of representative women, and the stained-glass presentations of Scripture characters and female virtues, seem to link it to the past; the energy and enthusiasm of its Principal, and the full tide of life that pulses through the whole, assure its place in the future of girls' education.

CHAPTER III

LIGHT IN DARK PLACES

THE fifties had witnessed the rise of these earliest colleges, and given hope to a little band of reformers whose efforts on behalf of light and progress were the chief feature of the sixties. Never was a reform happier in its advocates. Frances Buss, dreaming, while yet in her teens, of giving to future generations of girls that public school life which had been denied to her; Anne Clough, recording in her early diary the longing to do her country some great service; Emily Davies, devoting all her thought and energy to making that dream of a women's college a reality; Dorothea Beale, struggling against opposition and prejudice to build up the wonderful organisation at Cheltenham—these were some of the pioneers whose names have become as household words, whose portraits hang in many a home even beyond the seas, the patron saints of our girl students.

Side by side with these worked others, both men and women, who had come to realise the deplorable condition of girls' education. On the one hand, complaints were heard of their incompetence in domestic matters. 'They cannot keep house accounts,' says one writer; 'they neither can make puddings nor direct servants in making them; they cannot make or mend their clothes; in a sick-room they are either so nervous or so senseless that their presence is worse than useless.' On the other, we hear of the terrible strain consequent on what was by curious irony called over-education—girls sitting at their books or piano from morning to night, loading their memories with undigested facts. Both evils proceeded from the same cause. 'Everything that is taught is taught dogmatically, and consequently the powers of research, inquiry, analysis, and reason either are altogether crushed out or rust from want of use.'[11]

At this time public schools for girls were practically unknown. Teaching was no profession for women—it was the acknowledged resource of the middle-aged spinster left penniless by her father, or the widow whose husband had made ducks and drakes of the money. It was the one thing that anybody could do, since it required neither knowledge nor experience. All that was necessary was to hire a house, with a little saved or borrowed capital, and put up a brass plate on the door, announcing the existence of a select establishment for young ladies. Each schoolmistress did what seemed good in her own eyes or those of her pupils' parents, and though, when the principal was herself a cultivated woman, she often inspired her pupils with a love of books that remained with them in after years, these cases were the exceptions. The condition of the great mass of cheap day-

[11] *Examiner.*

schools was deplorable.

An attempt to penetrate beyond these brass-plated doors was made by Madame Bodichon, who as Barbara Leigh Smith had attended some of the earliest classes at Bedford College. The results of her inquiry were given to the Social Science Congress at Glasgow in 1860. She strongly denounced the little cheap private day-schools, academies, and such like, 'often conducted by broken-down trades-people, who failing in gaining a livelihood in a good trade, take in despair to what is justly considered, in consequence of the competition of the schools assisted by government, as a very bad business.' Happily, times have changed, and we can afford to smile at the picture of these 'genteel' establishments, with their 'insufficient room and ventilation,' where the young ladies were taught about the 'four elements, earth, air, fire, and water,' and, shutting their eyes and their windows, studied the wonders of nature in little cheap catechisms.

Some test for distinguishing good schools from bad ones seemed desirable in the best interests of teachers and pupils. In 1857 and 1858 Oxford and Cambridge had instituted local examinations for young persons not members of the Universities. These had proved useful in raising the standard of middle-class education, giving an aim and a stimulus to small schools. Why not do the same for girls? It was decided to make the attempt. In October 1862 a small committee was formed in London, with Miss Emily Davies as secretary. Permission was asked and given to conduct an informal examination for girls with the same papers as were set to the boys. The examiners looked over the answers and reported on them. The results were somewhat startling. Out of forty senior candidates thirty-four failed in preliminary arithmetic. The juniors did a little better. The average work in English was pronounced fair, and in grammar very good. French did not compare unfavourably with the boys. In German only twelve candidates presented themselves; all passed—three with distinction. Not such a bad record after all, but of course it was only the progressive schools that were represented. These learned that they must look to their arithmetic, and they did so with excellent results. Both the successes and the failures showed the value of the experiment, and it was resolved to repeat it. A memorial was sent to the Vice-Chancellor of Cambridge, signed by more than a thousand persons engaged in teaching or interested in education. The result was the formal admission of girls to these examinations. In 1865 they were held at six places: Brighton, Bristol, Cambridge, Manchester, London, and Sheffield. A hundred and twenty-six candidates entered; ninety passed. A great advance had been made in two years. Arithmetic was no longer a stumbling-block. Out of the whole number of candidates only three failed in it. English history came in for a share of praise. 'The examiners thought the style of the girls' replies better than that of the boys.' 'The answers of the senior and junior girls were orderly and methodical, and the writing and expression good. The papers of many gave proof of care and ability on the part of both teacher and scholar,' and more to the same effect. In 1866 there were two hundred and two girls at ten centres. This time the report was even more satisfactory.

These results were most valuable. They proved that there must be many good schools in the country, and some teachers who could learn from the success and failure of their pupils. No time could have been more opportune for this experiment, for just then a Royal Commission was making an inquiry into all the schools that had not been included in the Popular Education Commission, or that which examined into the nine great public schools. This really meant a general survey of boys' secondary education; and to boys it would have been confined, had it not been for those same energetic women who had inaugurated the reform of girls' education. Here was an opportunity not to be missed. Once more signatures were collected for a memorial, this time to beg for the inclusion of girls' schools in the scope of the inquiry. This was granted, and consent given to the admission of a few ladies to give evidence. Some trepidation was felt at so novel a proceeding. Thirty years later, when another such Commission was appointed, and women were included among the Commissioners, their appointment caused less remark than the invitation given in 1865 to a few ladies to give information on a subject on which none were better qualified to speak. So quickly has public opinion changed!

Nine ladies gave evidence before the Commission. The most valuable testimony came from Miss Buss, at that time head of a large private school, Miss Beale, Principal of Cheltenham College, and Miss Emily Davies, who was taking so active a part in all reforms that concerned girls. Eight Assistant Commissioners were requested to make special inquiries as to the girls' schools in selected districts. Their task proved no easy one. The request to be allowed to inspect schools or procure information about them by other means was met sometimes by indignant refusal, at others by a silence as eloquent. However, in spite of difficulties, it proved possible to obtain returns from a good number and examine some more or less thoroughly. Since the assumption seems fair that it was the superior schools which were most ready for inspection, the reports must be read with the mental addition of an even worse state of things behind that remained unrevealed. At any rate, there was enough to make out a case for action.

The report which was issued in 1867 summarised the impression formed by the Assistant Commissioners. 'It cannot be denied that the picture brought before us of the state of middle-class female education is, on the whole, unfavourable. The general deficiency in girls' education is stated with the utmost confidence, and with entire agreement, with whatever difference of words, by many witnesses of authority. Want of thoroughness and foundation; want of system; slovenliness and showy superficiality; inattention to rudiments; undue time given to accomplishments, and those not taught intelligently or in any scientific manner; want of organisation—these may sufficiently indicate the character of the complaints we have received in their most general aspect. It is needless to observe that the same complaints apply to a great extent to boys' education. But, on the whole, the evidence is clear that, not as they might be but as they are, the girls' schools are inferior in this view to the boys' schools.' Mr. Norris, one of the Assistant Commissioners, says: 'We find, as a rule, a very small amount of professional skill, an inferior set of school-books, a vast deal of dry, uninteresting task-work, rules put into the memory with no explanation of their principles, no system of examination worthy of the name, a very false estimate of the relative value of the several kinds of acquirement, a reference to effect rather than to solid worth, a tendency to fill or adorn rather than strengthen the mind.'

There is unanimous testimony as to the undue amount of time given to accomplishments, music in particular. There are some elaborate calculations as to the total number of hours spent on acquiring a mechanical skill on the piano, though about a third of the pupils never make the slightest use of it after they have left school. The music played is bad; there is little training for the taste and none for the mind in this study to which girls devote almost as much time as their brothers do to classics. Next to music modern languages absorbed most of the time and energies of the pupils, and yet the Commissioners unanimously report with severity on the results attained. Very few girls could compose a French sentence correctly; slipshod grammar and bad pronunciation are noted, and set down to the habit of speaking French out of school hours, by which a sort of jargon was developed incomprehensible to an outsider, and not even up to the standard of Stratford-atte-Bowe. On the subject of Science Mr. Fitch wrote: 'Few things are sadder than to see how the sublimest of all physical sciences is vulgarised in ladies' schools. No subject, if properly taught, is better calculated to exalt the imagination and to kindle large thoughts in a pupils mind. Yet all the grandeur and vastness are eliminated from the study of Astronomy as commonly pursued; and the pupils whose attention has never been directed to any one of the great laws by which the universe is governed, think they are learning astronomy when they are twisting a globe round and round, and solving a few problems in latitude and longitude.'

Arithmetic comes in for the worst censure. It is spoken of as 'the weak point in women teachers.' 'It would be an affectation of politeness,' says Mr. Hammond, to say a word on behalf of the arithmetic taught by ladies. It is always meagre and almost always unintelligent.' The school-books receive almost unqualified abuse, in particular *Mangnall's Questions* and 'all the noxious brood of catechisms.' History and 'miscellaneous subjects' are too often taught from these, geography and grammar from wretched little text-books, all the sciences in the course of a few lectures. Now and then a word of praise is given to English literature and composition, *e.g.*, 'English literature occupies a more prominent position in the education of girls than of boys.... The object of the lessons is to exercise the memory and to cultivate the imagination of the scholars; their most beneficial result is observable in the style of composition acquired by girls at a comparatively early age. Whereas a boy of fifteen hardly ever succeeds in putting together half a dozen readable sentences, a girl of the same age often writes with much freedom and fluency.... A bundle of letters written by girls of seventeen or eighteen afforded me real pleasure; many of these were well conceived and well expressed, and they presented a variety of style and subject which proved that they were not manufactured to order or cast in any stereotyped mould.'[12]

One of the most serious defects is the lack of all physical training, while attempts are made to combine exercise and instruction, *e.g.* by repeating French verbs when out walking, thus achieving neither result satisfactorily.

Not only were the Commissioners of one mind in their strictures, but there is a striking unanimity about their recommendations. Mr. Giffard's lucid summary

[12] Mr. Hammond's Report.

may be taken as also representing the views of his colleagues: 'If I were to sum up the impression I derived from my visits to girls' schools, I should say, (1) that the mental training of the best girls' schools is unmistakably inferior to that of the best boys' schools; (2) that there is no natural inaptitude in girls to deal with any of the subjects which form the staple of a boy's education; (3) that there is no disinclination on the part of the majority of teachers to assimilate the studies of girls to those of boys; (4) that the present inferiority of girls' training is due to the despotism of fashion, or, in other words, the despotism of parents or guardians.'

There is a general consensus of opinion on the following points:—

1. Most girls' schools are too small.

'There is little life, no collective instruction, and nothing to call forth the best powers of either teacher or learner in a school where each class consists of two or three pupils only.'—(Mr. Fitch.)

2. They lack proper organisation.

'There is a certain number of classes or of girls learning particular things, but there is neither any definite course of studies nor any grouping of classes, so as to play into one another.'—(Mr. Bryce.)

3. Want of proper proportion in arranging subjects.

4. Poor quality of the teaching, due to the inferior education of the teachers themselves.

5. Lack of an external standard to act as a stimulus to the learner and help to the teacher.

Mr. Bryce's recommendations are of special interest, since they mark out the lines on which the chief reforms have proceeded. They are these:—

1. The establishment of schools for girls under proper authority and supervision. 'It would be at all events most desirable to provide in every town large enough to be worthy of a grammar school a day school for girls, under public management, where a plain, sound education should be offered at the lowest prices (from £5 per annum or upwards) compatible with the provision of good salaries for teachers, and which should be regularly examined by competent persons thereto appointed.'

2. Considerable changes in the course of instruction for girls of all classes. 'It would be proper to lay more stress upon arithmetic, to introduce mathematics everywhere, and Latin where there is a fair prospect of a girl's being able to spend four hours a week upon it for three years.'

3. The foundation of institutions which should give to women the same opportunity of obtaining higher education which the Universities give to boys. The lack of this higher training injures the school education by lowering its tone, and opening up no wider field of knowledge to the more studious and eager scholars. An even worse result is 'the low standard of education and of knowledge about education among schoolmistresses and governesses.'... 'It is from the advent of more highly educated teachers that the first improvement in the education of girls

is to be hoped for.'

Such was the verdict of this famous Commission, whose 'revelations' have figured in so many prizegiving speeches. The report filled twenty stout volumes, which were duly relegated to their place on official shelves, to accumulate dust; and there, thirty years after, they have been joined by the nine volumes drawn up by our latest educational Commission. Truly has it been said that the best way to shelve a question in England is to let a Royal Commission sit upon it. But even a Royal Commission and a twenty-volume report could not shelve the subject of girls' education; the reformers were too much in earnest. Miss Beale extracted from these ponderous blue tomes all that related to girls, and reprinted it in a compact little volume. Even before its appearance action had been taken. The Cambridge Local Examinations had drawn schoolmistresses together and given them a common interest. They now began to form associations in different parts of the country. One was started in London, with Miss Buss as President and Miss Davies as Secretary. The North of England proved a specially congenial sphere for this form of union. The Ladies' Honorary Council of the Yorkshire Board of Education was an outcome of the introduction into that county of the Local Examinations, but it soon extended its operations over wider fields, *e.g.* domestic economy and sanitary science, as well as the extension of endowments to girls.

Even more far-reaching in its results was the North of England Council. This too originated in Schoolmistresses' associations, among which Miss A. J. Clough was a moving spirit. In 1865 she contributed to *Macmillan's Magazine* an article setting forth certain schemes for improving girls' education. One of these was to establish in other large towns courses of lectures similar to those given at Queen's and Bedford Colleges, to be attended by the older pupils from schools and by teachers. Co-operation between several towns would make it possible to engage really able lecturers from Oxford and Cambridge. The experiment was first tried at Liverpool, and spread to Manchester, Leeds, and Sheffield. Associations were formed in these four towns, and by the election of two representatives from each, the 'North of England Council for Promoting the Higher Education of Women' was constituted in 1867, with Miss Clough as secretary and Mrs. Butler as president. The lectures proved a phenomenal success. In the autumn of 1868 the numbers of the combined audiences in nine towns amounted to 1500, and Mr. F. Myers writing of them in *Macmillan,* enumerated their advantages thus:

'1. They contain within themselves the germ of university extension.

'2. They confront young women in a reasonable manner with reasonable men.

'3. They encourage and help governesses, who attend in large numbers, and are glad to have good teaching and to know of the best books.

'4. They form a nucleus for educational libraries and for the friendships of fellow-students.

'5. They pay.'

These lectures were in actual fact the beginning of University Extension, but the work of the North of England Council did not stop here. A further aim for study was needed, and some more advanced examination than those for girls under eighteen, if women were to be qualified to instruct girls in anything but elementary subjects. A petition was drawn up and sent to Cambridge with the signatures of over 600 ladies engaged in teaching, 300 interested in it, and six members of the late Schools' Inquiry Commission. They pointed out 'the great want which is felt by women of the upper and middle classes, particularly by those engaged in teaching, of higher examinations suitable to their own needs.' The petition was granted, and the first Women's Examination held in 1869.

Looking back on these past days now that it is the fashion to decry examination as the death of education, it is interesting to realise what this much abused system really did to give it fresh life. The Cambridge Senior and Junior Locals were the first link established between girls' schools and the university, and it would be difficult to over-estimate their value in this period of chaos. Their utility was recognised at once. They spread all over the country and to the colonies; and they are widely used by schools, both public and private, and by children working with governesses at home. Edinburgh and Durham soon followed suit in the admission of girls, and in 1870 Oxford too relented. London did its part by instituting a special Women's Examination on the lines of Matriculation, and in 1869 that of Cambridge was held for the first time. These were the germs of future developments. At London the way was paved for opening the degrees to women; the Cambridge Women's Examination led to the foundation of Newnham.

To some extent the work of these examinations is done. Conditions have changed; and the establishment of the Oxford and Cambridge Joint Board, and the opening of the universities to women have removed the necessity for this kind of examination in schools of the first grade. But in small private, and in middle-grade schools, and for children working with governesses at home, they are still of distinct use, and their popularity does not seem to diminish, if numbers are any test. Should they ever become needless, owing to a more perfect school organisation, we must still hold their memory in respect, for they can show a good record. It is their merit that at a time when no schoolmistress had a College training and no University examiner ever entered a girls' school, they supplied a slender link between the school and the university, and when there was no standard for girls' education, and often neither organisation nor curriculum, they did afford an aim and a stimulus, which, if not absolutely the best, proved at any rate trustworthy guides. If examination is not education it has often led to it, and never more successfully than in the case of girls and women.

CHAPTER IV

THE HIGH SCHOOLS

THE Report of the Schools' Inquiry Commission in 1867 served as a revelation, for it brought home to the general public the exceedingly unsatisfactory condition of middle-class education for both boys and girls. Its immediate outcome was an examination and redistribution of endowments, in which for the first time the claims of girls were considered. But it was evident that even the most judicious application of existing endowments could not suffice to fill all the educational gaps in the country. The Commissioners had therefore included among their recommendations the following:—1. To offer proprietary and private schools the same inspection and examination as were required in public schools, and to make their position more assured by a system of school registration. 2. To give power to towns and parishes to rate themselves for the establishment of new schools. These suggestions remained a pious opinion, for no action was officially taken, but (as so often happens in England) private enterprise stepped in, and compensated for public laxness. The inquiry had done good service in throwing light on the inefficient condition of small and cheap private schools for girls, of which there were such large numbers in the country. Clearly what was wanted was a system of schools large enough to permit of low fees and satisfactory grading. Much of the evidence had been negative, and showed what to avoid. Happily there were a few schools in existence which could serve as beacon lights. Of these the North London Collegiate and the Cheltenham Ladies' College took the first rank. The former, though really a large private school, had been organised by Miss Buss on public lines, with a view to being ultimately placed on a sound and permanent footing. The latter was a large proprietary school, so planned as to be in no need of public money. Both Miss Buss and Miss Beale were unanimous in urging the establishment of large public schools for girls. Speaking of London, Miss Buss had said, 'I think, in the first place, there are scarcely any good schools; in the next place, there are very few good teachers; and in the third place, there is no motive offered to the girls for study nor to their parents to keep them at school.' Miss Beale considered that schools were preferable to private teaching at home, because one person could not be mistress of all the subjects to be taught, 'and a good teacher can scarcely continue so when condemned to the monotony of the ordinary private school-room.' Small schools could not be properly graded except when very high fees permitted of small classes.

Large day-schools with low fees for girls were called for. This much was agreed on, but where was the necessary capital to be found? Among the public-spirited men and women who set themselves to answer this question, the foremost place belongs to Mrs. William Grey. She had for some time been working to get a share of educational endowments for girls. 'Let me remind you,' she wrote at this time, 'that while there are in or near London alone the magnificent first-grade endowed schools for boys of the Charterhouse, Merchant Taylors, St. Paul's, Harrow, and Eton, besides King's College and University College schools, there is not in the whole of London an endowed school of a similar class for girls, and that while the proportion of educational endowments for girls to those for boys is as 1:92, the proportion of women supporting themselves is to men as 1:7.19; that is, to quote the words of Mr. William Brook, "seven times as many men are employed as women, but men have ninety-two times as much money as women, to arm, equip, and qualify themselves for the battle of life."'

Failing endowments, or even side by side with them, capital must be obtained from other sources: this was the problem which had now to be faced. On May 31st, 1871, Mrs. Grey read a paper before the Society of Arts on the Education of Women. She described its extremely unsatisfactory condition, and suggested three remedies. (1) The creation of a sounder public opinion respecting the need and obligation of educating women. (2) The redistribution of educational endowments so as to give a fair share of them to girls. (3) The improvement of female teachers by their examination and registration according to fixed standards.

In the following October, at the Social Science Congress at Leeds, she proposed the establishment of a national Union for the improvement of the education of women of all classes. Its objects should be—(1) To enlighten the public mind, through meetings and lectures throughout the country, on the present state of female education, on the national importance of improving it, and on the measures required for that end. (2) To collect and disseminate information respecting the best methods of education, the comparative advantages of large and small schools, the influence of endowments, and generally all questions connected with the training of girls. (3) To promote measures for the better training of female teachers, and especially for their examination and registration by fixed standards, so as to secure a measure of competency. (4) To assist the formation of councils similar to the North of England Council for the Education of Women in other divisions of the country, and, while endeavouring to multiply local centres of activity, to afford all workers in the same cause a common bond of union, and a means of intercommunication and combined action.

The proposal was favourably received; 300 names were at once given in for membership, and a provisional committee formed. Individual subscriptions were fixed at five shillings; and an affiliation fee of not less than a guinea annually entitled corporate associations to be represented on the annual general council, and to all the privileges of membership. This National Union supplied a real need. Members poured in fast. The Princess Louise consented to become president, and the roll of vice-presidents was a distinguished one. Branch unions were formed, and associations already existing at Belfast, Dublin, Birmingham, Cambridge, Clifton, Falmouth, Guernsey, Huddersfield, Norwich, Plymouth, Northampton, Wakefield, Winchester, and Windsor were brought into membership with the Union.

Many of the Schoolmistresses' Associations sought affiliation: the Ladies' Council of the Yorkshire Board of Education, and the North of England Council also joined the Union, and consented to appoint representatives to the central committee. With admirably organised machinery directed by knowledge and enthusiasm, great reforms seemed possible, and in 1872 the Union proceeded to its first piece of constructive work, the establishment of the Girls' Public Day School Company.

Proceedings were inaugurated at a meeting at the Albert Hall, with Lord Lyttelton in the chair. Proposals were brought forward for starting a shareholding company 'for the purpose of establishing and maintaining in London and the provinces superior day-schools, at a moderate cost, for girls of all classes above those provided for by the Elementary Education Act.' A capital of £12,000 was to be raised in 2400 shares of £5 each. The proposal found favour, prospectuses were sent out, accompanied by a letter from Princess Louise; 800 shares were at once taken up, and the company was floated. Among the earliest members of its council were the Marquis of Lorne, the Dowager Lady Stanley of Alderley, Sir J. K. Shuttleworth, Mrs. William Grey, Miss Mary Gurney, and Miss Shirreff, Sir Douglas Galton, K.C.B., and Mr. C. S. Roundell.

The next step was to open schools, and Chelsea was chosen as the scene of the first experiment. Miss Porter was appointed head-mistress, and a suitable house was hired. The school began with twenty-five girls, and rapidly increased. A few months later a second one was opened at Notting Hill with Miss Jones as head. For these first experimental schools no shares were specially taken up in the neighbourhood. In future, any place that wished for a high school was usually required to take up a certain number, as a definite assurance of local interest. Croydon was opened on these conditions in 1874, with twenty pupils. Then followed, in 1875, Clapham, Hackney, Bath, Oxford, and Nottingham; in 1876, Brighton, Gateshead, and St. John's Wood; in 1878, Dulwich, Ipswich, Maida Vale, Sheffield. At present the schools number thirty-four. They are at Bath, Blackheath, Brighton, Bromley, Carlisle, Clapham (High and Modern), Clapton, Croydon, Dover, Dulwich, Gateshead, Highbury, Ipswich, Kensington, Liverpool, East Liverpool, Maida Vale, Newcastle, Norwich, Nottingham, Notting Hill, Oxford, Portsmouth, East Putney, Sheffield, Shrewsbury, South Hampstead, Streatham Hill, Sutton, Sydenham, Tunbridge Wells, Wimbledon, York.

The fees are: for pupils under ten years of age, £10, 10s. a year; entering the school between ten and thirteen, or remaining after ten, £13, 10s. a year; entering after thirteen, £16, 10s. a year. The company is on a sound financial basis, since the larger and more flourishing schools make up for the deficiencies of the smaller ones. Until 1896 a dividend of five per cent. was paid, now limited by resolution of the shareholders to four per cent. The capital has been increased to £150,000.

Meantime similar schools were springing up all over the country. At Plymouth one was started by a local branch of the National Union, at Huddersfield by a local company, at Southampton by the Hampshire Association, at Manchester by private subscription, at Bradford by an endowment. The impulse given by the Union and its pioneer schools was felt everywhere, and it seemed as though before long every large town in England would have a proprietary or public school for girls. A rival company was founded in 1883. The Church Schools Company differed from the Girls' Public Day School Company in making definite Church teaching one of its objects, while the religious instruction of the Girls' Public Day School Company had always aimed at being, as far as possible, undenominational. The promoters of the Church Schools thought that as there was room for voluntary schools side by side with board schools, so there might also be scope for Church High Schools in spite of the existence of the Girls' Public Day School Company. Their original proposal was to start schools of various grades for boys and girls above the class attending elementary schools, where a general education should be given, in accordance with the principles of the Church of England, at a moderate cost.

A beginning was made with day-schools for girls, and hitherto little else has been done. It is probable that this Church Company did, to some extent, meet a need, but it was not a very large one. The majority of the Church of England parents are perfectly satisfied with the religious instruction of the Girls' Public Day School Company schools, and the new schools drew their pupils, not so much by an appeal to those who disapproved on principle of the existing high schools, as by establishing themselves in towns which the other company had not entered. Naturally they appealed to a smaller class, and can never expect to attain the numbers of the undenominational high schools. Hence they have always been, to some extent, hampered, for though the company is financially sound, and gives a small dividend to shareholders, it has had to economise very severely in the matter of salaries and buildings. This must always re-act to some extent on the education, and it is probably for this reason that these Church Schools have never attained the high position of their rivals. The fees paid vary according to the locality, some being as low as £4, 4s., others as high as £18, 18s.; £9, 9s. to £12, 12s. seems the commonest fee. Many of the schools are very small. At present the number is twenty-six, and they are situated at Bournemouth, Brighton, Bury St. Edmunds, Derby, Dewsbury, Durham, Gloucester, Guildford, Hull, Kendal, Kensington, Leicester, Newcastle-on-Tyne, Northampton, Reading, Reigate, Richmond, St. Albans, Streatham, Stroud Green, Sunderland, Surbiton, Wigan, Woolwich, Great Yarmouth, York.

High Schools can now trace back their history for a quarter of a century. In that time more than a hundred have been founded in England. They have become the typical girls' schools of this country, private schools have been organised on the same lines, and the scheme of large day schools with no distinction of class, giving a good education at a low fee, has been almost universally accepted. It seems so simple and natural, that it is hard to realise that twenty-five years ago it was a strange and therefore a dangerous innovation. After all what do we mean by a High School? There is a general impression of the meaning of the term, though it would not be easy to define it. In the United States, a High School is an advanced school, which can only be entered by pupils who have already passed through the Primary and Grammar Schools; that is, do not enter before the age of fourteen or fifteen. It is thus a Secondary School, forming the link between the primary institutions and the University. Our English High Schools provide both elementary and secondary instruction, and the ages of the pupils range from seven to nineteen.

Hence, although there is a natural division between the Lower and Upper School, the work is closely connected; the same mistresses teach in both, and subjects such as Latin and French are usually carried down into the lower classes. The lower part of a High School is not exactly parallel to an Elementary School; the pupils have begun more subjects, they have been taught in smaller classes, and by different, less rigid methods. The High School cannot therefore at present be regarded as the middle rung of the educational ladder. In England there is a gap between it and the Elementary School, which is sometimes successfully bridged by special means, but the existence of which cannot be disregarded in any general scheme of English education. As the need of secondary education is more generally felt, a system of schools leading upward in direct line from the elementary school is being naturally evolved, and connection between the two lines is being provided by scholarships and other means. But if we disregard a few exceptional cases, it seems best to look on the High School as an organic whole, taking the child from the nursery to the university, and sometimes even helping out the nursery by means of the kindergarten.

It is not uncommon to hear people talk of the High School system, but this is misleading. In so far as the High Schools have a special system, it is the natural outcome of the scheme of large classes and careful gradation. Hence it resembles in many respects that which has long prevailed in Germany and the United States. There is no High School Code, and even under the same management, *e.g.* in the Girls' Public Day-School Company Schools, considerable latitude is left to the individual head-mistress; but there are certain arrangements which are found convenient in the organisation of large day schools, and which prevail with modifications in all the High Schools, as well as in many large private institutions.

The morning hours are given to class teaching; from 9 to 1, or 9.15 to 1.15, being the usual times. Subjects requiring individual instruction (which are usually extras), *e.g.* piano, solo singing, advanced drawing, and painting, are taught in the afternoons, also Greek in some schools, special coaching in advanced Latin or Science, and so forth. The principle underlying this arrangement is that of giving the best working hours to serious mental work, and reserving accomplishments which are rather the ornament than the essentials of education, for the latter part, thus assigning to the subjects of instruction their proper relative importance, and keeping the real work of the school undisturbed. This arrangement seems so easy and natural that it would be hardly necessary to dwell on it, were it not that until very lately the opposite system prevailed in some schools that otherwise aimed at thoroughness, and it was not unusual for a girl to be called away in the middle of an important lesson in history or arithmetic, and sent to her music. Under the present plan, the greater part of the girls have finished their school work by one o'clock, and have the afternoon and evening free to divide between preparation of lessons (two to three hours), exercise, and home duties. For the benefit of those who require help in their lessons, or cannot get a quiet room at home, a system of afternoon preparation at school is organised. This generally lasts an hour and a half to two hours—most schools provide a dinner for girls who come from a distance. A whole holiday on Saturday seems the rule everywhere.

Some schools have a kindergarten department attached, where little boys are taught along with the girls, and a transition class where the children learn to read before passing into the school proper. The division is into forms, I. being the lowest, and VI. the highest. Large schools divide the forms into Upper and Lower. Where a school is fully organised, it is usual for a whole class to move up together. Backward girls may remain in the form another year. Unfortunately many high schools are too small to be fully organised, and in these the gaps between the classes are too large, and general promotion impossible. Clever girls spend one year in a class, slower ones two, and the disadvantage for the latter is very serious, since there is a weariness about going over the same ground twice, which is the reverse of stimulating. Large classes can progress as quickly as smaller ones when they are very carefully grouped. Where the pupils are at different stages there is much waste of time, and either the weak go to the wall, or the strong get less than their due. It is, therefore, the first essential of a high school that the numbers should be large, not much under two hundred.

Even when the school is large and the classes work smoothly together, the girls do not all work evenly in every subject. To prevent waste, it is usual to let certain subjects, perhaps Arithmetic and English, determine promotion, and to teach the others in divisions. Two or three forms may take French at the same time, and be rearranged for that lesson, returning to their own rooms when it is over. This moving about affords a pleasant change, and is quite easy when the building is a convenient one. Indeed, suitable premises are almost as important for the harmonious working of a school as large numbers and careful classification. Long narrow corridors and awkward staircases are fatal to order. Ordinary dwelling-rooms adapted for school purposes can seldom be properly ventilated, and according to their position in the room, the pupils suffer from draught or heat, the light falls the wrong way upon their work, the classes have to be graded to suit the size of the rooms rather than the abilities of the pupils. In fact nothing can be more unsatisfactory than the adaptation as a school of an ordinary dwelling-house.

The arrangement that seems to answer best is that of a large central hall used for prayers and general gatherings, out of which some of the form-rooms open, whilst the rest, with extra rooms for small divisions, are upstairs. Of this construction the Blackheath and Sheffield High Schools are good examples. The finest girls' buildings are naturally found where there is an endowment, as at the North London Collegiate, the Bedford, and Manchester High Schools. Few, if any of the Church schools have specially constructed buildings, and several of the Girls' Public Day School Company's Schools are carried on in adapted premises. Some grant of public money for buildings to really efficient proprietary schools would probably be the cheapest and most effective way of helping girls' education in many of our large towns.

The North London Collegiate, both in point of time and in importance, claims precedence as the pioneer high school. It was in working order when the Girls' Public Day School Company started, and was doubtless the model set before its promoters. The following account written in 1883 by Mrs. Bryant, who is now head-mistress, is in many ways typical, and applies *mutatis mutandis* to the general routine of all fully equipped high schools.

'Entering the school with the girls in the morning, we should proceed first through the entrance hall down to the basement, and into the cloak-rooms. Here each girl has a numbered place provided with hooks for cloak and hat, umbrella-stand, boot-rack, and bag for the house-boots, which she always wears while in school. There are also shelves for books while dressing is going on, and forms for use in changing boots. Since the space allotted is ample, and the girls come in relays, both before and after school, crowding is avoided.

'When ready, each girl goes upstairs with her books to the great hall, where the rule of silence is strictly enforced. At 9.15, all are assembled for prayers, each form in its place, while the prefects, who are members of the sixth form, and are elected by it and the teachers of the upper division of the school, are scattered among the other forms, as guardians of public order, during the interval of waiting. After prayers, each form marches out with its mistress to its own room. Five class-rooms open out of the hall on the ground floor; these are used by the upper division of the school, including the sixth form, and four sub-divisions of the fifth form. Five more open out of the hall gallery, used by all the sub-divisions of the fourth form, which constitute the middle division of the school. Above these two tiers, there is a third set of rooms, three class-rooms and the drawing school. The lower divisions of the school use these four rooms, besides one of the irregularly placed rooms. Of the latter there are several, lying with the laboratories, lecture-room, libraries, and music-rooms, on the side of the great stone staircase, opposite the Clothworkers' hall.

'Each class room contains 5600 cubic feet, and is fitted for thirty-two girls. All have Swedish desks, except the elder girls, who have separate desks with chairs. There is a raised platform for the teacher, with a chair and table. All the rooms are fitted with cupboards, and in most there is a small circulating library, which the girls can use on payment of a small subscription. The pine wainscot, brick walls, and tiled fire-places of the class-rooms, make a good background for the decorations of the Kyrle societies, which exist in each class; and all the rooms have pictures on the walls, as well as notice-boards and time-tables. Another institution of the decorative kind is the window garden, with which many of the rooms are provided, and in which the girls take, for the most part, great pride.

'In these rooms the hard work of the day goes on till 1.30, with an interval, as near the middle as possible, of twenty-five minutes, for a light lunch and drill. In five separate relays, the girls proceed to the dining-hall, which, with the kitchens and housekeeper's room, lies under the great hall. Here they can buy buns, biscuits, bread and butter, fruit, coffee, milk, and lemonade, and, while talking as loudly and as much as they please, they are required to take their stand in orderly lines across the room. From the dining-hall the girls proceed to the gymnasium, a very fine room, 100 feet long by 30 feet broad, where they have musical drill for a quarter of an hour. Monday and Thursday, however, are days for special calisthenic exercise, lasting half-an-hour each day. Then work is resumed till 1.30, when the school is dismissed in relays, as before stated.'

Even more important than the routine of a school is its curriculum; and here the need of the reformer's hand is still felt acutely. The subjects included in the Girls' Public Day School Company prospectuses are the following—Religious Instruction, Reading, Writing, Arithmetic, Mathematics, Book-keeping, English grammar, composition, and literature, History, Geography, French, German, Latin, the elements of Physical Science, Social Economy, Drawing, Class-singing and Harmony, Gymnastic Exercises, and Needlework. To these Greek must now be added, since it is taught in every school that prepares for college. The prospectus says 'any or all of these may be taught,' which means that the head-mistress has, within certain limits, a right of selection. Hence the tendency of schools, even under the same management, to vary greatly. Not only is there as yet no consensus of opinion in England as to the best curriculum for girls' schools, but even the general aim to be kept in view seems by no means determined. Mrs. Bryant lays down the incontrovertible dictum that 'the ideal of the curriculum is a balance of subjects so that all normal faculties and interests may be cultivated.' But there is another side which cannot be neglected, and the claims of the ideal vanish into insignificance before the demands of practical life and outside examination. In spite of the repeated promises that examination is to be servant and not master we must not hope to escape from its dominion as long as it is the 'open sesame' of colleges and professions. A rough test, it is still the best hitherto devised, and serves on the whole to separate the sheep from the goats. Since we must, therefore, acknowledge its sovereignty, it behoves us to see that it exercises a wise and benevolent tyranny. However much we may protest, the curriculum of a school will always be largely determined by the nature of its leaving examination, since this regulates the work of the upper forms, and these more or less mould the lower. Some schools reduce this examination work to a minimum, reserving it entirely for the highest form, while others use the machinery of outside examinations to determine the whole of their work. The North London Collegiate belongs to this latter class. The upper part is organised according to two parallel courses. Of these *A.* leads to the London degree examinations, that is to Matriculation or in some cases Intermediate Arts, and Course *B.* to the Cambridge Senior and Higher Locals. All these examinations under certain conditions admit to the Women's Colleges at Oxford and Cambridge, and hence act the double part of a leaving and entrance examination, but this school also makes use of the lower examinations, *e.g.*, the Preliminary and Junior Locals. Hence the work of these classes must be directed to the set subjects required for these examinations, and must include the particular periods of history, works in literature, and French and German books that are laid down by the examiners, even though they may not seem the most suitable in other respects. Many educationalists think this disadvantageous to the general plan of a girls' school, which should proceed on stated harmonious lines from the lowest to the highest class. Mrs. Bryant, however, thinks that the advantages outweigh the disadvantages, since 'by their means the more advanced body of opinion can be brought to bear on the inert or prejudiced mass, which lags behind in the movement of educational progress.' In spite of this valuable testimony the consensus of opinion is rather on the other side. The schools of the Girls' Public Day School Company have almost entirely abandoned the miscellaneous junior examinations, which lead to nothing, in favour of those conducted by the Joint Board of Oxford and Cambridge. This is the test applied to the leading boys' public schools since 1873, and it is the nearest approach in England to an *Abiturienten* examination, since the higher certificate, if taken in the required subjects, exempts its holder from the first public examination at Oxford and Cambridge. The Board awards higher and lower certificates, and undertakes a general examination of the schools. The papers are sent to the school, and the examination is conducted there under the supervision of the head-mistress. The lower forms are also examined *viva voce* by a delegate of the Board, and reports on the general condition of the school and on the paper work are sent to the governing bodies. In this way the progress of different schools can be compared, and a general control kept, while there is little disturbance to the school course, since the questions are set on the work actually done. The Council of the Girls' Public Day School Company itself awards certificates to girls who gain sixty per cent. of the marks in five papers.

The subjects of the higher certificate examination are arranged in four groups:—

GROUP I.

(1) Latin. (2) Greek.
(3) French. (4) German.

GROUP II.

(1) Mathematics (elementary).
(2) Mathematics (additional).

GROUP III.

(1) Scripture Knowledge. (2) English.
(3) History.

GROUP IV.

(1) Natural Philosophy (Mechanical Division).
(2) Natural Philosophy (Physical Division).
(3) Natural Philosophy (Chemical Division).
(4) Physical Geography and Elementary Geology.
(5) Biology.

All candidates for a higher certificate must satisfy the examiners in at least four subjects taken from not less than three different groups, unless they take one subject in II. or IV., in which case they can choose three from I. No one may offer more than six subjects. The examination is so arranged as to hamper the school work as little as possible. Thus in languages great stress is laid on grammar, composition, and unprepared translation, while the set books can be selected from a long list; or (to give even greater freedom) it is allowed to 'substitute with the consent of the Board other portions or periods which are at least equivalent to those specified in the prescribed list, provided that the extra expense involved be defrayed by the school authorities.' This privilege of choice is extended also to Scripture, English and History.

The subjects for the lower certificate are:—

GROUP I.

(1) Latin. (2) Greek.

(3) French. (4) German.

GROUP II.

(1) Arithmetic.

(2) Additional Mathematics.

GROUP III.

(1) Scripture Knowledge. (2) English.

(3) English History. (4) Geography.

GROUP IV.

(1) Mechanics and Physics.

(2) Physics and Chemistry.

(3) Chemistry and Mechanics.

The higher certificate is often taken by girls in Form Lower VI., and they are then free in their last year to prepare for university scholarships or do other special work. The lower certificate is less popular, but it is sometimes taken in Form V.

Unquestionably the real problem before our girls' schools is to plan a curriculum which, while keeping in view the harmonious development of mind and body, and the preparation for a girl's future life, shall yet give the necessary preparation for these final examinations. The reformers see hope in a more careful grouping of studies which shall break down the barriers between them, so that the subjects learnt at the same time should be allies rather than rivals. If fewer were taken up simultaneously, more time and interest might be given to each new requirement when it first appears on the scenes. After a couple of years, when considerable advance had been made, it might be relegated to a less important place and a fresh central study chosen. In the higher forms the threads would be once more drawn together, for then a pupil must be prepared to marshal all her forces for one great occasion. Experiments of this kind have been tried with much success in America, and there is a scheme for doing something of the kind in England. There is a plentiful field for experiments, and no doubt the curriculum question will be discussed at many a teachers' meeting before the problem is solved. The High Schools will contribute their share to the work if they are to remain in the van as they have hitherto done.

Since the very establishment of the High Schools was a protest against the superficiality and showiness condemned by the Royal Commission, their main endeavour was to avoid the mistakes of their predecessors. Accomplishments were relegated to the background. Arithmetic and mathematics were taught for their mental training and the development of accuracy. 'The noxious brood of catechisms' was abandoned in favour of a system of oral teaching: object lessons were introduced into the lower forms to induce observation, and in the science lessons facts were taught first-hand and not through the medium of books. The slipshod French chatter of the boarding-schools gave way to stricter grammatical training; parsing and analysis took the place of rote repetition of the parts of speech. Accuracy and thoroughness were the aim everywhere. At first the instruction was attended with many difficulties. There were few well-educated and no trained teachers, and very little agreement as to the really best methods. Hence it was natural that the revolt against the abuses of the past should produce some fresh faults. The reaction against the old text-books caused the introduction of a lecture-system; an excessive amount of note-taking, writing out, and correction by the teacher seemed to afford both parties the maximum of effort with the minimum of result: books were shunned as though the printed word were in itself hurtful, and much matter was laboriously dictated that might have been taken from any intelligent hand-book. The girls spoiled their handwriting, instead of straining their memories; that was the chief difference. Happily this plan has given way to more intelligent inductive methods, though even now there is a tendency in some schools to rely too much on written notes and too little on training the attention and memory. High School girls still need to learn how to use a book intelligently, and to appreciate knowledge that comes to them in an unaccustomed fashion. They have learnt the use of writing, to make 'an exact man,' but reading as a means of producing the 'full' woman has hardly as yet touched the High School system. This defect is now being realised and efforts will doubtless be made to remove it. Already the improvement in the teachers has produced a beneficent revolution in girls' schools. To their inadequate education the Royal Commissioners largely attributed the unsatisfactory state of things they found. Side by side with the growth of the high schools went the movement for admitting women to the universities, both acting and re-acting on each other, since the high schools sent up their best pupils to college and the college sent them back to teach and train future students. A great proportion of the mistresses are now university women, while a smaller number have been trained at the Cambridge Teachers' College or the Maria Grey or other Training Colleges—Kindergarten Colleges provide teachers for the little ones.

While the High School puts intellectual subjects first, it does not disregard accomplishments, though it seldom uses that word. Music is taught to all in the form of class-singing; piano and violin and solo singing are 'extras,' and do not belong to the general school work. Drawing has really won a more important place than before, because it is used as an educational factor, and not merely for purposes of show. The scheme of the Royal Drawing Society, organised by Mr. Ablett, is in use at nearly all the high schools. It is essentially a class system, and aims at training the eye, hand, and memory, rather than producing mere technical skill. The little ones in the first form are taught to present graphically objects interesting to themselves, by means of simple ruling, memory, and brush-work exercises. Special features are judgment at sight, memory and dictated work, the early introduction of drawing from objects and simple geometrical design. The schools are examined once a year. The examination takes place in the school itself under the superintendence of the head-mistress and drawing teacher, the work is sent up to London, and promotion to the next division depends upon the pass. Pupils who pass all the six divisions with honours are entitled to a full Drawing Certificate which has a commercial value for teaching purposes. Drawing, a little modelling, and needlework in the lower forms, represent at present the manual side of High School teaching. Cookery, dressmaking, etc. though popular in a different class of school, have hardly as yet been able to effect an entrance, nor does it seem altogether desirable that they should. That every school cannot teach everything is an axiom long ago accepted for boys' education, and it must be realised for girls too, if the outcry against overstrain is to cease. Differentiation is the only safe course. It is partly the strength and partly the weakness of the High School that it represents, in fact, two schools: the first grade for girls who are to proceed to the university, and whose life at home makes a certain amount of literary and linguistic attainment desirable, and the second grade for those who must leave at fifteen or sixteen, and look forward to a career in business or to practical utility at home. In the lower forms the need of both is the same: a good general education; afterwards bifurcation seems desirable. When a school is not large enough to allow of this, it is the early-leaving girls who go to the wall. For these an entirely different scheme of education might be best—this too is a problem that will have to be faced. Physical training is also considered at most of the High Schools. Generally, fifteen minutes in the middle of the morning is given to some form of drill. In a few large schools, *e.g.*, the North London Collegiate, this daily drill is undertaken by a specialist. Usually it falls to one of the assistants, though it is very common for a special teacher of Swedish drill to visit the school once or twice a week, and take all the girls in divisions. The North London Collegiate and the Sheffield High School have gymnasiums, and take this side of the work very seriously. A physical-record book is kept, and every child on entering is examined by a lady doctor attached to the school. Particulars of sight, hearing, throat, breathing, lungs, heart, chest, and waist measurement are recorded, with any observations considered necessary. Suitable gymnastic exercises are then prescribed, and the examination repeated from time to time, and note made of any changed condition. Some such plan might be tried in all High Schools, were the parents willing to pay for it. The low fees charged cannot be expected to include medical supervision as well as all the other advantages. At present Sheffield and the Camden Schools are almost the only day-schools that consider the physical training as systematically as the intellectual. Still, the Girls' Public Day School Company has now appointed a qualified lady inspector of physical training. Exercise doubtless plays an important part in every high school, but it is sometimes pursued with more zeal than knowledge. Just now athletics are taking a very prominent place. School playgrounds and playing fields have become a necessity. Girls have learned to play cricket, hockey, and rounders; they choose their elevens, elect their captains, and have their practices and matches much like their brothers. How far this particular kind of exercise is conducive to a girl's health is another of the still unsolved problems. One thing is certain: these games do much to improve the general tone of a school. Their effect in producing loyalty and public spirit and promoting cheerfulness is quite as marked in girls as in boys, and the development of the play side, along with the greater liberty, the giving of responsibility as a reward, and all that belongs to a real public school are features at least as valuable as the improvement in the teaching. The High Schools have produced a new type of girl, self-reliant, courageous, truthful, and eager for work. A full record of their after careers would prove interesting. Many pass straight from school to Oxford or Cambridge, a great many have gained scholarships, and the women's colleges are largely recruited from their ranks. Some pass on to the medical schools, others gain County Council scholarships for technical or scientific work, large numbers are engaged in teaching, one or two have taken up gardening at Swanley Horticultural College, and a good many are making themselves generally useful at home as wives or daughters. Almost everywhere the High School girl proves herself capable, accurate, and trustworthy. She is sometimes blamed for a want of grace, such as belonged to a few rare ladies of the olden time, but she also lacks the helplessness and silliness that were prevalent then. Physically, morally, and intellectually, these schools may claim that they are improving large numbers, and with them surely the race.

CHAPTER V

ENDOWMENTS FOR GIRLS

THE history of endowed schools carries us far away into the misty realms of the past, before ever the Conqueror set foot in England and put back the clock of civilisation a hundred years. The earliest schools of which we have any knowledge were attached to the chief collegiate churches, where one officer would be specially told off to teach the boys, just as another would conduct the singing. Convent and school or church and school were invariably allied. The first separable school endowments were merely assignments of a specific part of the general endowment for the support of the chancellor or his deputy, the grammar school master. Like the earliest colleges these schools were founded 'for prayer and study.' The first person to reverse this order, and endow an independent school, was William of Wykeham, when in 1393 he founded Winchester College, to give free instruction to seventy poor boys, and so help them to holy orders or the university. Thus the new school became 'a sovereign and independent corporation existing of, by and for itself, self-centred, self-controlled.' 'To make education, and that education not the education of clerics in theology or the canon law, the paramount and pronounced object of an ecclesiastical institution, with all the paraphernalia of Papal bull and royal and episcopal license, was no small innovation. It was a new departure, which opened a new era in the world of education, and therefore of thought.'[13] Later founders, following in the steps of William of Wykeham, gave sums of money for the training of youth in 'grammar and good manners.' Grammar meant Latin and Greek, the 'key to all the sciences'; the manners were to be those of a true gentleman, 'trouthe and honour, fredom and curteisie.'

Following on these came the schools of the Reformation age, of which the most familiar example is Dean Colet's foundation of St. Paul's. These were established or assisted by the gifts of 'pious founders,' or sometimes by diverting old funds originally destined for other purposes. Reading school was founded out of funds obtained by suppressing an almshouse for poor sisters, and under Elizabeth made into a grammar school 'for educating the boys of the inhabitants of the said borough and others in literature.' Such schools were often placed under lay control, but the clerical idea was still in the background. Not priests, but ministers of the reformed religion, were needed, and learning became even more essential for men who had to make knowledge take the place of tradition.

The clerical purpose of most of these schools naturally tended to exclude girls or make them of secondary importance. What place was actually assigned to them

[13] A. F. Leach.

in the 353 schools founded between the accession of Henry VIII. and the death of James I. is a problem that must be left to antiquarians. Certain it is that in the ensuing period the education of both sexes was more on an equality, since the standard was one of inferiority. An age of political disturbance was followed by an epoch of frivolity. Learning fell into contempt. The foundations of the eighteenth century were not grammar but charity schools, and though girls were not forgotten, it was with the hope of training servants for themselves that rich persons supported these schools. Not to give a liberal training, but to teach the poor to 'keep their proper station,' was the aim of eighteenth century founders.

Thus it came about that the Schools' Inquiry Commissioners found a goodly number of girls in endowed schools of an elementary character, which would hardly bear comparison with the poorest of our modern board schools. While the King Edward Schools at Birmingham were giving 290 boys a classical and 300 a sound English education, none of these benefits fell to girls. In the elementary schools of the same foundation were 655 boys and 630 girls. At Christ's Hospital, distinctly founded for both sexes, there were but 18 girls as against 1192 boys. Perhaps even the eighteen would have been better off elsewhere. They occupied a part of the junior boys' school at Hertford; they had one ward under the charge of a nurse, their playground was a little over a quarter of an acre, they took their walks abroad under care of the nurse, they had no calisthenics or other physical training; their diet was bread and milk for breakfast, bread, meat, potatoes, and porter for dinner, bread and butter, milk and water for supper. There was no admission examination, no leaving standard of attainment; they learned a little Scripture, English (so-called), and History and Geography from abridgments. On leaving, at about fifteen, most of them were apprenticed to business. It did not prove easy to place them. No wonder!

A similar tale might be told of Bedford School. It was established in 1566 by Sir William Harpur and Dame Alice, his wife, 'for the education, institution, and instruction of children and youth in grammar and good manners, to endure for ever.' Did child mean 'boy' in the minds of the founders? It seems uncertain; for, as the endowment increased in value and some of it became available for purposes other than the free grammar school, the interests of girls were also considered. At various periods of the eighteenth century fresh uses were found for the surplus money, and it is characteristic of the age that the feminine equivalent for a sound education was a dowry. £800 a year was set aside for marriage-portions for forty poor maids of the town of Bedford, to be distributed by lot, provided that a successful candidate was married within two calendar months of drawing the lot, and not to 'a vagrant or other person of bad fame or reputation.' Naturally there was not much difficulty about claiming the lot. Young men came from far and near to woo the 'maids of Bedford.' Any residue was given to poor maid-servants who had resided five years at Bedford and were married within a year. The next addition was a hospital for boys and girls, an allotment of £700 to apprentice fifteen boys and five girls, and almshouses for ten old men and ten old women. Early in this century preparatory and commercial schools were added; and girls were considered to the extent of a foundation where the head-mistress received £80 per annum as against the headmaster's £1000. Which figures very eloquently sum up the relative estimation in which girls' and boys' education was held before 1848.

The Schools' Inquiry Commission had made it abundantly clear that the educational endowments of the country needed overhauling. Not only had many of them increased greatly in value, but the establishment of public elementary schools was making the appropriation of endowments for elementary schools unnecessary. Again, many free schools were giving a liberal education to the sons of rich men. By the institution of even a low fee considerable sums would become available for the improvement of existing schools and the establishment of new ones. Then there were the various charitable endowments left for special purposes which no longer existed. In some cases money had been bequeathed to the poor in a parish, and was simply used for the relief of the rates. In London alone there were sums of £1500 a year given for the relief of poor prisoners from debt. Among other out-of-date purposes were the ransom of Barbary captives, the destruction of lady-birds in Cornhill, etc. In a certain part of Worcestershire money had been left in 1620 for distributing bread among the poor of seven parishes and, as a secondary purpose, supporting a free grammar school, the surplus to be applied to repairing the church and bridges, and increasing, if expedient, the salary of the schoolmaster. By 1867 the total income had increased to £657, and was applied to elementary schools and a free grammar school for fourteen boys. In other cases money was left for doles; with the result that in a certain parish, too richly endowed, extra waiters had to be put on at the gin-shops for two weeks before and after the distribution. In fact it was a case of money in the wrong place; education starving for want of funds that were only doing mischief. The regulation of the educational charities, and appropriation of those others which were doing more harm than good, was becoming an urgent necessity. Some changes had already been made under the Charitable Trusts Acts, but these were a good deal limited in their operations, and a more systematic reorganisation was undertaken under the Endowed Schools Act of 1869. This appointed three commissioners for four years to inquire into the endowments of England and Wales, and the first to hold this office were Lord Lyttelton, Canon Robinson, and Arthur Hobhouse, Q.C. In 1874 this Commission was merged in the Board of Charity Commissioners for England and Wales.

'In framing schemes under this Act, provision shall be made as far as conveniently may be for extending to girls the benefits of endowments.' This clause is the Magna Charta of girls' education, the first acknowledgment by the State of their claim to a liberal education. This result was in great part due to those same men and women who had brought about the opening of the local examinations, and induced the Commission to take cognisance of girls' schools, and were striving, in face of all opposition, to win something like a university education for girls. As early as 1860 at the Social Science Congress Madame Bodichon had entered a strong protest against the theory that boys' education must be assisted and girls' self-supporting. 'Magnificent colleges and schools, beautiful architectural buildings costing thousands and thousands of pounds, rich endowments all over England, have been bestowed by past generations as gifts to the boys of the higher and middle class, and they are not the less independent and not a whit pauperised.' At first this was but a voice crying in the wilderness, but the cry was taken up first by a few supporters, then by the whole country, and at last the *Times*, certainly not a revolutionary organ, declared that, 'This country is most abundantly and redundantly endowed for men and boys, as if they were unable to take care of themselves, whereas there is little—indeed nothing, we may almost say—for that which is contemptuously called the weaker sex.'

An Association for Promoting the Application of Endowments to the Education of Women was formed, and offered to assist trustees of schools and other persons interested in education by supplying information and suggesting plans whereby available funds might best be applied to the education of women. It had a strong committee, which numbered among its members Miss Davies, Miss Clough, and Miss Bostock, as well as Mr. Bryce and Mr. Fitch, those constant and helpful supporters of all efforts to improve the education of girls. At this time the needs of the middle class seemed most urgent, since the State-aided schools were coming to the aid of the very poor, and the rich could pay the high terms that were then demanded by the better private schools. The immediate need seemed to be for schools of the second or third grade, *i.e.* those meant for girls who would leave school some time between fourteen and seventeen, and might be expected to pay fees ranging from £4 to £10 per annum.

Of such schools the first were founded out of the surplus revenues of King Edward's Schools at Birmingham. Here four schools of the second grade were opened, each to accommodate about 160 pupils. These not only filled at once, but had to refuse admission to 500 candidates. In 1870 the Grey Coat Hospital at Westminster was opened; but on the whole progress was slow, and Mr. Roundell's estimate in 1871 that there were in England and Wales 225,000 girls waiting for secondary education was probably not wide of the mark.

In that same year an event occurred of far-reaching importance. The admirable institution so long associated with the name of Miss Frances Buss was transformed into a public school for girls. Readers of her interesting biography now realise, what had long been known to her friends, with what a single mind and earnest devotion she had worked for the cause nearest her heart—the establishment of public schools for girls. As early as 1850, her own private school had been reconstituted on public lines, with the help of the Rev. David Laing, one of the promoters of Queen's College, but her ambition was to make it public in fact as well as in its methods. Attention had been drawn to her work by her evidence before the Schools' Inquiry Commission, and now some of its members themselves came forward to help her. If ever a school could lay claim to public aid, it was this one; and as soon as the enabling act was passed, active measures were taken to secure for it an endowment. With rare clear sight Miss Buss realised that a fully equipped school can only be self-supporting by the sacrifice of either suitable buildings, adequate salaries, or a scale of fees suited to the neighbourhood. She wanted to organise a pioneer school in which none of these good things should be lacking; nothing less than the best seemed good enough. Her enthusiasm and confidence were not to go unrewarded. In December 1870, a public meeting was held in the

St. Pancras Vestry Hall, to announce the formation of a trust for carrying on the existing school, and starting another of a lower grade in connection with it. The upper school thus constituted took the name of the North London Collegiate, and in January 1871 removed with its two hundred pupils to 202 Camden Street, and at the same time the Lower or Camden School came into existence. According to Miss Buss's principle, the fees under the new trust were calculated to meet current expenses only. The building was to be provided from other funds, as was done in boys' public schools. A subscription list was opened, and every possible endeavour made to win public support. These were anxious years for Miss Buss; money came in slowly, and rather than abandon her principle she chose to sacrifice her salary. Nor did she wait in vain; the excellent work of the school won it recognition, and when in 1874 the Charity Commissioners were called upon to dispose of the Platt Charity derivable from property in St. Pancras, belonging to the Brewers' Company, they recommended that £20,000 be given to the North London Collegiate and Camden Schools. Thus building funds were secured, afterwards supplemented by a generous donation from the Clothworkers' Company. The scheme became law in 1875, and the two schools have continued since then to work side by side as endowed schools of the first and second grade, with different principals, but both under the superintendence of the head-mistress of the upper school. This arrangement has proved most valuable, as it promotes co-ordination instead of rivalry between the two schools. In other places where two grades exist side by side, it is not uncommon to find the lower one attempting with inadequate means to imitate the upper. The special needs of the class attending it are then neglected, and undue attention given to a few clever girls, for whom leave is sometimes obtained to stay beyond the appointed age. At the Frances Mary Buss Schools (as the two are now called in memory of their founder), this danger is obviated by a good system of scholarships from the lower to the upper.

At the Camden School girls may attend from seven to seventeen. The fees range from £5, 2s. to £8 per annum. The subjects taught are the usual English ones, with Class-Singing, Needlework, Drawing, and Book-keeping, and the elements of Science. Special attention is given to theoretical and practical Domestic Economy, and these classes receive assistance from the London County Council. French is the only foreign language taught. At the North London Collegiate, girls may attend between eight and nineteen, the list of subjects is much wider, and selections have to be made under the direction of the head-mistress. French, German, Latin and Greek, are included in the curriculum, and the practical subjects either omitted or reduced to a minimum. Since the work of the school is directed to the London University Examinations and the Cambridge Higher Locals, the course is necessarily laid out for girls who can stay long enough to enter the upper forms, and perhaps proceed to college. The fees range from £17, 11s. to £19, 14s. But girls over sixteen proceeding from the lower to the upper school pay only £14, 8s. Many pass up by means of scholarships.

These two schools with their thousand pupils, fine buildings, and noble roll of honours won by old pupils stand pre-eminent among girls' endowments. The principle that with a scale of fees adapted to meet current expenses the endowment should provide buildings and scholarships has been triumphantly vindicated by the Frances Mary Buss Schools.

Almost simultaneous with the endowment of these schools was the appropriation of some part of the funds of the Bradford Grammar School, 'to supply a liberal education for girls by means of a school or schools within the borough of Bradford.' Public opinion was, however, hardly ripe for such a diversion of any large part of an old endowment, and although, as Mr. Forster pointed out at the inaugural meeting, a charter of Charles II. had assigned the land 'for the better teaching, instructing, and bringing up of children and youth,' 'which terms are of common gender,' the money assigned to the girls would not have been sufficient to start the school, but for the generosity of the Ladies' Educational Committee, which raised a sum of £5000 for purchasing the buildings. Thus the Bradford Girls' Grammar School came into being. The fees are £12 to £15, 15s., and girls may stay till eighteen or nineteen. It is thus technically of the first grade, and as such prepares the pupils in the highest class for the university. Many, however, leave school long before attaining this stage, and this appears to constitute one of the special difficulties of North of England schools. There is, however, a wide list of subjects which may be taught, and from these the head-mistress arranges each pupil's curriculum. As the fees are the same as those of a high school, the endowment fund helps to supply better salaries, apparatus, etc. and thus to increase efficiency. A scholarship fund of £1000 has been provided by the generosity of two private donors, and forty-one scholars have by its help already proceeded to the university.

Manchester also has a first-grade endowed school, which originated like so many others in those active years that followed 1870. Here too the initiative was taken by an association for promoting the higher education of women. The school was started in 1873 by subscription, and in 1876 the present site in Dover Street was secured for building, and over £5000 raised for the purpose. A few years later, an opportunity occurred of securing some public money, as the wealthy foundation of Hulme's Charity was to be reorganised. The school secured a share, receiving a capital grant of £1500, and £1000 a year on condition that the governing body should be reconstituted to give it a more representative character. Under the new arrangement, there are representatives of the Hulme Trustees, Oxford, Cambridge, Victoria, and London, Owens College, and the Manchester School Board, as well as other co-opted members. This representative character has proved of the greatest value to the school, which takes rank as one of the first in the country. The buildings are admirable in convenience and arrangement, and the scholarship fund amounts to £640 a year. Two smaller schools lately established by the governors at Pendleton and North Manchester have somewhat diminished the numbers of the parent school, but prove a boon to girls in those parts, since the means of communication at Manchester are somewhat inadequate. Only Manchester girls are received in the High School, or those residing with near relations. There are no boarding-houses; it is a purely local school. The fees are nine to fifteen guineas per annum. Manchester has been specially successful in 'assimilating' those girls that enter the high school from the elementary schools, several of whom have passed on to the university with scholarships, and been very successful in their after careers. Its chief want is a system of scholarships from the elementary schools, to enable it to extend its useful work, and take a place in a national system of education.

The most complete schemes of endowed schools for girls are at Birmingham and Bedford, and they are typical of two different systems. The King Edward's endowment, one of the largest in England, had been so mismanaged that in 1828 only 115 boys were being educated on it, and the school building was in ruins. In 1831 by a Chancery scheme, two new schools, Classical and English, were established, and twenty years later there were sufficient funds to maintain eight elementary schools as well. Immediately after the passing of the 'Endowed Schools Act' further changes were made. The schools were reorganised in three grades (high, middle, lower middle), and four grammar schools founded for girls. When the spread of State-aided elementary schools made the third class unnecessary, these were abolished, and a girl's High School substituted. This forms the last link in the chain; and a close connection between different grades by means of scholarships, leading gradually upward from the elementary school to the university, gives the necessary cohesion to the system. The High School can accommodate 260 girls, and the four grammar schools 780. Fees are charged in all, but not so high as to cover the cost of education. At the High School it is calculated that the expense of each pupil is £20 per annum, while the fee is £9. The endowment makes up the deficiency, and permits the reservation of one-third of the places for foundation scholars. Further, it enables the governors to offer their teachers good salaries, and to conduct the whole on those generous lines without which it is impossible to provide a liberal education for either girls or boys. In educational organisation as in municipal matters, Birmingham is a model to the rest of the country. It shows how an old endowment, sufficiently large and carefully distributed, can be made to meet the needs of all classes of a community. 'We cannot reform our ancestors,' as George Eliot so pertinently remarks, nor can we set down rich old endowments in the midst of places that have never known such benefactions. But fresh money is coming in from new sources, and we want object lessons in its application. Birmingham teaches the value of co-ordination, and incidentally the use to which public funds may be put in bringing a good education within the reach of the largest possible number.

The position of Bedford is different. A small town with no special industry happens, through the munificence of one of its ancient citizens, to be possessed of one of the largest endowments in the kingdom. For many years its benefits were confined to the inhabitants of Bedford, and as a result the population was constantly increased by persons who were glad to get free education for their sons. Many, no doubt, were well able to pay for it, but preferred, naturally enough, to get it for nothing. At the time of the Schools' Inquiry Commission, the endowment was maintaining:—(1) A grammar school with 204 boys. (2) A commercial school with 358 boys. (3) A preparatory commercial school with 237 boys; as well as elementary schools for nearly 1200 children and a hospital for 13 boys and 13 girls, almshouses, etc. Considerable as were these numbers, they fell far short of the possibilities of the endowment. The institution of a fee, even a low one, would at once set free a goodly sum, and something, if only as compensation for the marriage portions, was due to the girls. A new scheme providing for a fresh distribution of the funds was drawn up in 1873, but the girls' schools did not come into existence till 1882. Under the present arrangement one-eleventh of the available funds is used for eleemosynary purposes, two-elevenths go to the elementary schools, which until quite lately have served all the needs of the town and rendered a schoolboard unnecessary. The remainder is divided equally between the two higher schools—boys' Grammar and girls' High—and the two Modern schools. This looks very much like putting girls and boys on an equality, but a clause in the scheme explains that three boys are to be considered equal to five girls. In other respects the money is evenly divided; it is shared out annually 'in proportion to the average number of scholars attending the said schools respectively during the preceding year,' a curious application of a Scriptural doctrine, by which a rise in numbers in the boys' school entails a corresponding deficit in the exchequer of the girls' school and *vice versa*. Still, rightly managed, there is enough for all.

At Bedford no attempt is made to co-ordinate the work of the two schools, or to establish any but the very slightest connection—by means of a few scholarships—between the elementary and modern schools. Hence the benefit of co-operation is lost. The great difference between the fees—£9 to £12 at the High, £4 at the Modern school—makes active rivalry impossible. It is the state of the home exchequer that settles the choice of a school, far more than the preference for one system of education or a girl's probable after-career. It is curious that, in spite of the general outcry for cheap schools, the low fee of the Modern School has not proved as great an attraction as was expected; it has filled but slowly, and is only now approaching 200, while the High School averages an attendance of 600. To some extent the curriculum of both schools is the same, but the greater economy requisite in the Modern school necessitates larger classes, less complete equipment, and lower salaries for the teachers. To families in straitened circumstances, local shopkeepers, and small farmers within a short train journey of the town, the school is a great boon; but it seems certain that at Bedford, whatever may be the case elsewhere, all who can afford the higher fee are willing to pay it for the sake of the greater social prestige of the High School. Prejudice of this kind must always be reckoned with, however carefully Parliament or Royal Commissioners may provide on paper for the needs of each class of the population.

On the other hand, the High School has more than fulfilled anticipations. Not only does it provide a first-class education for the sisters of grammar school boys, it has won a position and prestige of its own which attract considerable numbers from a distance. There are now several flourishing boarding-houses, all working in close connection with the school, and under the superintendence of the head-mistress. In this way Bedford High School, like the Cheltenham Ladies' College, St. Leonard's School at St. Andrews, and a very few others, has taken a position somewhat analogous to that of a boys' public school, sought for its own sake, and not merely on account of its nearness or cheapness. The large numbers, ample staff, and sufficient funds enable the head-mistress to consider the needs of individual pupils more carefully than could be done in a small school. Forms are joined and subdivided lengthwise and crosswise, so as to bring together in small groups girls who are to give a good deal of time to Classics, Modern Languages, English, Drawing or Science, or any other special subject, thus avoiding the scrappiness with which the modern curriculum is sometimes charged. The girl who aims at the university is prepared for it, the girl who has a real taste for accomplishments receives first-rate instruction in music, drawing, etc. and at the same time is encouraged to give special attention to English. There is no attempt to force all through the same mill. The school is most fortunate in its buildings, which are beautiful as well as convenient. Hall, gymnasium, studio, laboratory, padded rooms for practising, nothing seems wanting to the equipment. It is pleasant to wander through the airy and tasteful class-rooms and realise that this is one of the many good things which the redistribution of endowments has given to girls. At Bedford there is not much risk of forgetting whence the money comes. The Harpur Trust seems to give its character to the town. The numerous schools, the Harpur Trust offices, the rows of almshouses, the 'Harpur' and 'Dame Alice' streets are suggestive of a town that has grown up about its schools, almost as Oxford and Cambridge have about their colleges. In the old church close by the founders lie buried; ever succeeding generations of boys and girls are entering into their inheritance.

Among the eight largest endowments of which the Commissioners had to take cognisance was that of Dulwich. In few places was the reformer's hand more needed than in the assignment of those large sums which had accumulated under the charity of Alleyn's College of God's Gift. At the time of the Schools' Inquiry Commission—that date which marks a new starting-point in educational chronology, it maintained only an upper school with 130 boys, and a lower school with 90. In 1895 when some of the results of twenty-five years were summarised, it was supporting:—(1) A first-grade boys' school—Dulwich College—with 630 scholars. (2) A second grade boys' school—Alleyn's School—with 540 boys; and contributing, (3) To James Allen's Girls' School a capital sum of £6000, and £650 a year. (4) To the Central Foundation Schools—boys and girls—a capital sum of £11,000 and £2300 a year. (5) To St. Saviour's Grammar School, Southwark, a capital sum of £20,000 and £500 a year.

This is a result that should please all parties. In spite of the additional advantages given to boys, the girls gain two schools; for although the James Allen school had been founded as early as 1741 by James Allen, master of Dulwich College, it was really nothing more than an elementary school until its reconstruction in 1882 with a part of the Dulwich endowment. It can accommodate 300 girls, has eight class-rooms, laboratory, assembly hall, dining-room, recreation ground of two and a half acres, and a completely equipped gymnasium where lessons are given by an expert teacher. With a £6 fee it is always full, and admirably serves its purpose of 'supplying to girls of the middle class a sound practical education.'

The fourth of the large endowments belongs to St. Olave's Grammar School, and a school for girls is in course of establishment here.

The Tonbridge endowment, administered by the Skinners' Company, now supports a school for girls at Stamford Hill.

The Manchester Grammar School fund has of late decreased in value, and has nothing to offer girls; but here they have had help from another quarter.

The Jones foundation at Monmouth now provides for 500 boys, and 100 girls, besides 50 elementary scholars, in place of 180 boys at the date of the Commission.

Of the eight endowments, by far the largest was that of Christ's Hospital, and here there was no question as to the original intentions. The treatment of girls had been so unfair as to arouse general indignation. But the whole foundation really needed overhauling. After long delays an elaborate scheme was drawn up, providing for the removal into the country of the boys' school, proper boarding-school provision for girls, and large day-schools in London for both sexes. Of all this, now nearly twenty years after the passing of the Endowed Schools Act, very little has been done, though the removal of the boys' school from London to Horsham is now definitely settled. At Hertford the girls' school has been reformed in its methods, and additional ward accommodation provided, but by a perverse system of election it is made very difficult to fill even that space. Girls can only be admitted on presentation of a governor—very difficult to obtain—or by a competition, to which only three classes are admitted. They must come either from—(1) Certain endowed schools in England and Wales, or (2) Public elementary schools in the London School Board district, or (3) Certain parishes which have hitherto exercised the right of presentation. As (1) and (2) represent the classes which are best provided, and least in need of the benefits of a cheap boarding-school, and (3) is, by its nature, very restricted, it is not strange that it has hitherto proved impossible to fill even the 140 available places, though there are thousands of girls in rural districts to whom a school of this kind would prove a priceless boon. There seems a curious irony about offering such nominations to the Bedford Modern School where girls are receiving an excellent education for £4 a year, and taking no thought for those less favoured places, which, because they have no endowment of their own, are therefore shut out from one that they could use. Of course all this is only temporary, but the transition stage seems a very long one. As far as girls are concerned, the chief needs seem to be the establishment of several cheap boarding-schools, the election of some women on the council of almoners, and a change in the present system of electing scholars. Let us hope that when the reforms come at last, they may prove to have been worth the waiting.

Besides these eight chief endowments, there are many others of which girls have now received a share. There are now in England and Wales over eighty girls' endowed schools of a secondary type, though the distribution is curiously uneven; *e.g.* the West Riding of Yorkshire has nine, while Surrey has only one. Much has been done, and much remains to be done, but it is well that every kind of experiment should be tried, so that the newer schemes may be improved by the experience of the older ones.

Endowed schools are technically supposed to be of three grades, according to the age at which the pupils usually leave. For the first the limit is eighteen or nineteen; for the second, sixteen or seventeen; for the third, fourteen or fifteen. All admit them at seven or eight. There is something peculiarly English about this arrangement, which, on paper at any rate, appears needlessly wasteful. The natural division seems the American one. Here there are three successive grades, organically connected, by which a child may go through his whole school career, passing, as it were, from the kindergarten at one end to the university at the other. This arrangement of schools, all free, and meant for all the children of the community, is in harmony with the American democratic idea, but would be impossible in the midst of English class prejudice. Still even our social exclusiveness does not require such extreme differentiation, and experience shows that a system of three parallel lines, distinguished chiefly by breaking off at different points, is not altogether necessary. The problem, as it presents itself for girls, is not, however, the same as for boys. Boys' schools of the highest grade naturally prepare their pupils for the university, and as most of them are boarding-schools, they are exempt from considering local needs. The first public schools for girls were day schools. At the time of the first Endowed Schools Act, university education for girls had hardly made any way. Girton was just struggling into existence, the other colleges were but a dream of the future. London still withheld its degrees. What girls needed most was a sound general education given cheaply in day schools. Hence the low fees fixed by the Girls' Public Day School Company, and the still lower ones charged at the endowed schools of the second and third grades, which at that time met the most crying want. By 1883 ten of these third grade schools in London were educating over two thousand girls. Among them were the Greycoat Hospital at Westminster, and the Roan School, Greenwich, and others that have since extended their sphere of work up to the second grade limit.

The course of events during the last few years has necessitated these and many other changes. The Elementary Schools Act of 1870, and the spread of Higher Grade schools, while largely removing the need for the third grade, have necessitated some means of transition from the primary to the secondary school. On the other hand, the rise of women's colleges, technical institutes, etc. and the increasing number of girls who, whether from choice or necessity, expect to earn their own living, necessitates a levelling-up of schools, and a closer connection with places of higher education. Direct connection with the primary schools on the one hand, and the women's colleges on the other, is now a necessity. Many of the Charity Commissioners' schemes have attempted to supply this. The Roan School at Greenwich is a good instance. It was founded in 1643 out of money left by John Roan to clothe and educate poor children, and reorganised in 1873, the income of £2000 being divided between 350 boys and 320 girls. There is a special fund for foundation exhibitions for elementary scholars, and others are admitted on passing an examination, at half-fees—£3 instead of £6. Of the total number of pupils, about two-fifths come from the elementary schools. Thus the work of the two is brought into very close connection, and the Roan School includes in itself both second and third grade functions. It provides for the upward passage by exhibitions, many of which are held at Bedford College, or in Wales.

Scholarships of both kinds are also given by the Skinners' School at Stamford Hill. Some of the entrance exhibitions are restricted to pupils from elementary schools, others are awarded by open competition. The two leaving exhibitions, of the value of thirty-three and thirty guineas respectively, are tenable for four years, at any place of advanced education approved by the governors. The school fees range from £6 to £10. The work of the Sixth Form leads to the higher certificate of the Joint Board or the London Matriculation, both of which serve the purposes of a leaving and entrance examination. This school might therefore be regarded as a combination of the three grades. Similar work is done by the Mary Datchelor School at Camberwell, the Aske's School, Hatcham, and several others. Such schools, with a definite connection upward and downward, are among the chief educational needs of the day. Those now at work seem to be always full, and they draw their pupils from a class that look forward to a career of steady work. Clerks, civil servants, teachers, typists, telegraphists, milliners, nurses; these, and many others, occur in the lists of old pupils' occupations. A useful general education, either as an end in itself or as a basis for higher or technical education, is given, and these schools have taken the place of the third rate private schools, which was all that had previously been offered to middle class girls. The expression of opinion by the Royal Commissioners, in 1895, that 'a second grade school, which prepares for the local University College is often more suitable for a certain section of the population than a first grade school linked to Oxford and Cambridge,' applies, *mutatis mutandis*, to girls as well as boys. For both, a part of the highest work must be supplied by boarding-schools.

But when all the endowments hitherto made available are considered, the share of the girls is still far too small. In some counties there is hardly anything available for them. Against this disparity must be set the benefactions of recent years, many of which are specially meant for girls and women. The foundation of the City of London Girls' School, by William Ward, in 1881, with an endowment of £20,000; the Pfeiffer Charity of £59,000, for the benefit of women's education, the numerous scholarships given by city companies, the establishment of Holloway and Westfield Colleges, and of many other foundations for both sexes, belong to the twenty years between 1875 and 1895. If girls have lacked much in the past, they are inheriting the present. As the Charity Commissioners remarked, when reviewing a record of a quarter a century: 'As to one particular branch of educational endowments, viz. that for the advancement of the secondary and superior education of girls and women, it may be anticipated that future generations will look back to the period immediately following upon the Schools' Inquiry Commission, and the consequent passing of the Endowed Schools Act, as marking an epoch in the creation and application of endowments for that branch of education, similar to that which is marked for the education of boys and men by the Reformation.'

CHAPTER VI

THE WOMEN'S COLLEGES

THE chief gain that this half-century has brought to women's education is their admission to the universities. It is the key-stone of the arch, without which the rest of the fabric could have neither stability nor permanence. The schools look to them for their teachers and their standard, and gain thereby an element of fixity hitherto lacking. If boys' education may be blamed for excessive conservatism, that of girls has suffered from extreme mobility. Since girls' schools led nowhere, and acknowledged no outside guidance, their aim was perpetually changing, according to the ever-varying dictates of sentiment or expediency. Independent and unorganised, they lacked all connection with past and future; and it is this that the universities are now giving them.

Apart from its intrinsic importance, this reform is remarkable for the speed and completeness with which it has been accomplished. Thirty years ago it had hardly been seriously contemplated; now eight of the ten universities of Great Britain teach their students without distinction of sex, while two others admit them to lectures, examinations, and many other privileges. All this has not been brought about without hard work and persevering effort; and it would be vain to seek the origin of all the separate forces that, acting and re-acting on one another, have produced this result. Many were the workers, and the honours of the pioneers must be shared, but among those who led the way a chief place belongs to Miss Emily Davies. From the first she realised that the reform in girls' education must begin at the top. To quote her own words: 'The incompleteness of the education of schoolmistresses and governesses is a drawback which no amount of intelligence and goodwill can enable them entirely to overcome. It is obvious that for those who have to impart knowledge the primary requisite is to possess it; and it is one of the great difficulties of female teachers that they are called upon to instruct others while being inadequately instructed themselves. The more earnest and conscientious devote their leisure hours to continued study, and no doubt much may be done in this way; but it is at the cost of overwork, often involving the sacrifice of health, to say nothing of the disadvantages of working alone, without a teacher, often without good books, and without the wholesome stimulus of companionship.'[14]

But, important as was the improvement in the education of the teachers, Miss Davies had a wider aim in view for the college she meant to found. It was to bring a really liberal education within reach of all women, apart from any special pro-

[14] Emily Davies, *Higher Education of Women.*

fessional aim. Girls, as well as boys, should have opportunities given them to carry on their studies in congenial and stimulating surroundings, unhampered by the cares of earning and unhindered by conflicting duties. To them, too, the college life was to bring that joyous spring-time of youth, friendship, and unfettered delight of study and leisure which had hitherto been withheld from them. Such was the generous purpose in the minds of a few men and women who were trying to fire others with their own enthusiasm.

Even at the time of the Schools' Inquiry Commission this question had been mooted, and a memorial had been sent up pointing out the want of a system of 'instruction and discipline adapted to advanced students, combined with examinations testing and attesting the value of the education received.' The report of the Commission and the discussion it aroused helped to give publicity to the proposal, and at last it was resolved to test the feasibility of the scheme by actual experiment. In 1867 a committee had been formed to consider the possibility of founding a college 'designed to hold in relation to girls' schools and home teaching a position analogous to that occupied by the universities towards the public schools for boys.' It was resolved to try an experiment on a small scale, and proceed further as funds became available. At Hitchin, near Cambridge, a small house was hired for the six students who presented themselves, and in October 1869 they began the work prescribed to candidates for degrees by the University of Cambridge. Insignificant as these beginnings may seem, they were of momentous importance in the history of women's education. The founders of this, the first women's college in England, had to choose once for all between a women's university, with its exclusive studies and degrees, and admission to the great universities of the country. The question of a women's university debated and vetoed in 1897 had really been finally settled in 1870, when the first lady students requested and received permission to be examined in the papers set for the Previous Examination.

The prospectus of the new college issued in the autumn of 1869 contained this clause: 'The Council shall use such efforts as from time to time they may think most expedient and effectual to obtain for the students of the College admission to the examinations for the degrees of the University of Cambridge, and generally to place the College in connection with the University.' This ambitious programme thus early laid down for the infant College must have provoked many smiles; and looking back now after the lapse of nearly thirty years, we hardly know whether to wonder most at the confidence placed by the founders in the hitherto untried abilities of girls or at the success which so abundantly justified their anticipations.

It was thus made clear from the outset that the new college was to be no self-centred institution, but was to derive its teaching, inspiration, and standard from Cambridge, provided always that the University were willing to accept the new responsibilities thus proposed. For this end it seemed desirable to make an informal experiment, and through the kindness of the individual examiners five of the students were submitted to the test of the Previous Examination. All were successful; four attained the standard required for a First Class, and one that of a Second. Two years later three students entered for Tripos Examinations in the same informal manner, two passing in classics and one in mathematics. Thus three years after the opening of the College three of its students had fulfilled all the conditions required by the University of Cambridge for a degree in Honours. That was a sufficient answer to the doubters; the founders had justified their action. Henceforth the future of the College was fixed.

Meanwhile vigorous efforts were being made to raise money for the permanent building to be erected in or near Cambridge. This was no easy task. Generous donations for the needs of women were at that time unknown. The *Quarterly Review* recommended 'simplicity of living and the strictest economy' as alone suitable for women who might have to earn their own living, and desired to combine with this 'training in housekeeping, regular needlework ... such cultivation as will make a really good wife, sister, and daughter to educated men.' Against such selfish and confused notions it was difficult to contend. As Miss Shirreff wrote at the time: 'Never yet have a company of women been able to scrape together funds for an object specially their own, be it club, or reading-room, or hospital, or, as now, a college.' It is pleasant to realise that this is no longer true, and that the writer of these despairing words lived to see the change she had helped to bring about.

The money came in, though slowly. Madame Bodichon generously gave the first thousand pounds, and among the earliest subscribers was George Eliot. Lady Stanley was another who gave liberal aid. The subscription list gradually grew longer; a piece of land was secured at Girton, near Cambridge, and building began. In 1873 it was ready for occupation, and henceforth became the home of the Ladies' College, now incorporated as Girton College, with Miss Davies installed as Mistress. As the numbers increased, fresh additions were made to the building, but the aim and work of the College remained unchanged. Students were prepared for the Ordinary and Honours Degree Examinations by means of lectures given at Girton, and, as these were gradually opened to women, by attendance at some of the professorial and intercollegiate lectures in Cambridge. They were informally examined with the same papers as were set to the men, and in every detail of preliminary test, length of residence, etc. they conformed to the rules laid down by the University for its members. In lieu of the degree, which could not be conferred upon them, they received from the College a 'degree certificate,' and year by year fresh proofs were given of the general efficiency of the College and its students. In this way informal connection with the University was combined with formal adherence to its regulations. Thus matters continued till 1881.

Side by side with the beginnings of Girton, another movement had been at work. This was largely due to the North of England Council, which by promoting examinations for women over eighteen, had been establishing a fresh link between the University of Cambridge and the education of girls. A Cambridge committee established courses of lectures in all the subjects of examination. These naturally attracted many students from a distance, and the same persons who had organised the lectures, soon had to face the problem of housing the audience. Mr. Henry Sidgwick, to whose generous and unfailing assistance women owe so much, invited Miss Clough to come and take charge of a house of residence for women students. This house—No. 64 Regent Street—became the germ of Newnham. As the numbers increased, removal to larger premises became necessary, and Merton

Hall was taken. When this too had to be abandoned it was resolved to build. Funds were raised by the Newnham Hall Company, and eventually this was amalgamated with the association which had charge of the lectures, and the two were incorporated as Newnham College. This development from small beginnings, under the Principal's able management with the constant help and sympathy of Mr. and Mrs. Sidgwick, has now been fully made known through Miss A. B. Clough's interesting biography of her aunt. Newnham has seen some changes of policy and programme since its first beginnings in 1870, but its true aim, to advance the education of women at Cambridge, has always remained the same.

Since Newnham originated in a house of residence for girls preparing for the Higher Local Examination, this was naturally the goal set before the first students; but very early in its history some few who were more ambitious or better prepared, found this aim insufficient, and began, like the Girton students, to study for the degree examinations. The Higher Local, at first the goal, gradually receded in importance, and became a preliminary instead of a final, but it was not made compulsory to follow the Cambridge curriculum exactly, and in those early days great latitude in choice of subjects, examinations, length of residence, etc. was allowed to Newnham students.

Thus matters continued till 1880, when special attention was called to Girton by the distinguished success of one of its students, who was declared by the examiners in the mathematical Tripos to be equal to the eighth wrangler. There was now a ten years' record of good work to show, and the time seemed opportune for bringing about a more formal connection with the University. A memorial was drawn up and presented, which called attention to the 'repeated instances of success on the part of students of Girton and Newnham Colleges, in satisfying the examiners in various degree examinations at Cambridge,' and praying the Senate to 'grant to properly qualified women the right of admission to the examinations for University degrees, and to the degrees conferred according to the result of such examinations.' This was signed by 8500 persons; other petitions to the same effect were received, and as a result a syndicate was appointed to consider the matter. Their report advocated the formal admission of women to the Honours examinations of the University, and the publication of a separate class-list, indicating the position of each in the general list. They did not, however, recommend conferring degrees on women, nor did they advise admitting them to the Ordinary Degree examinations. The recommendations were embodied in three Graces, passed by the Senate on February 24, 1881, a red-letter day in the annals of College women. These are the most important:—

'1. That female students who have fulfilled the conditions respecting length of residence and standing which members of the University are required to fulfil, be admitted to the Previous Examination and the Tripos Examinations.

'2. That such residence shall be kept—(*a*) at Girton College; or (*b*) at Newnham College; or (*c*) within the precincts of the University, under the regulations of one or other of these Colleges; or (*d*) in any similar institution within the precincts of the University which may be recognised hereafter by grace of the Senate.

'3. That certificates of residence shall be given by the authorities of Girton College or Newnham College or other similar institution hereafter recognised by the University, in the same form as that which is customary in the case of members of the University.

'4. That except as is provided in regulation 5, female students shall, before admission to a Tripos Examination, have passed the Previous Examination (including the Additional subjects), or one of the examinations which excuse members of the University from the Previous Examination.

'5. That female students who have obtained an Honour certificate in the Higher Local Examination, may be admitted to a Tripos Examination, though such certificate does not cover the special portions of the Higher Local Examination, which are accepted by the University in lieu of parts or the whole of the Previous Examination; provided that such students have passed in Group B, (Language): and Group C, (Mathematics).

'6. That no female student shall be admitted to any part of any of the examinations of the University who is not recommended for admission by the authorities of the College, or other institution, under whose regulations she has resided.

'7. That after each examination a class-list of the female students who have satisfied the examiners shall be published by the examiners at the same time with the class-list of members of the University, the standard for each class, and the method of arrangement in each class being the same in the two class lists.

'8. That in each class of female students in which the names are arranged in order of merit, the place which each of such students would have occupied in the corresponding class of members of the University shall be indicated.

'9. That the examiners for the Tripos shall be at liberty to state, if the case be so, that a female student who has failed to satisfy them, has in their opinion reached a standard equivalent to that required from members of the University for the ordinary B.A. degree.

'10. That to each female student who has satisfied the examiners in a Tripos Examination, a certificate shall be given by the University stating the conditions under which she was admitted to the examinations of the University, the examinations in which she has satisfied the examiners, and the class and place in the class to which she has attained in each of such examinations.'

This was followed in 1882 by permission to pass the examinations for degrees in Music.

The Colleges and their students thus received formal acknowledgment from the University, and the status then conferred remains unchanged to this day. Two attempts have since been made to induce the University to carry its concessions to their logical issue, and confer degrees on women. That of 1887 came to an untimely end, as it was not even considered by a syndicate; the events of 1897 belong to recent history, and are too fresh to allow a proper estimate of their significance. The facts are these. In 1896 four memorials were presented to the Council, asking for the nomination of a syndicate 'to consider on what conditions and with what restrictions, if any, women should be admitted to degrees in the University.' The syndicate was appointed, and reported in favour of conferring 'the title of the degree of Bachelor of Arts' by diploma upon women, 'who, in accordance with the now existing ordinances, shall hereafter satisfy the examiners in a final Tripos Examination, and shall have kept by residence nine terms at least; provided that the title so conferred shall not involve membership of the University.' This seemed a very moderate proposal, since it only involved a formal acknowledgment of privileges already conferred, but somehow the University took fright. Perhaps it now for the first time realised what had already been done, and determined to allow no more concessions; perhaps an element of jealousy was beginning to play a part among the younger members who had appeared in the same class lists as the women, and not always in the highest places; certain it is that while the best weight and learning in Cambridge were in favour of the proposals, numbers were ranged on the other side; and the voting resulted in a majority of more than a thousand against the proposal. In estimating this result it is well to remember that the women's colleges had met with far more rapid success than even their founders had anticipated. They had produced a Senior Wrangler and a Senior Classic, and a formidable list of first classes in these and other Triposes. It was no longer possible to put aside their achievements with the old contemptuous formula, 'very good considering.' The movement had succeeded beyond all hope or fear, and while its true friends remained staunch, many of the indifferent now ranged themselves among the open enemies. Events had moved too fast for the rearguard of public opinion to keep up with them. At any rate the refusal was decisive, and matters settled down once more to the *status quo* of 1881.

Anomalous as is their position, the students of Girton and Newnham have many and great advantages. For a comparatively low fee they receive all the advantages of a University education; they enjoy the manifold privileges that belong to residence in Cambridge, they may attend nearly all professorial and very many college lectures, their own colleges also provide excellent lecturing and coaching; and they may enter for any of the Tripos Examinations, and for those that lead to the degrees of Doc. and Bac. Mus. They have the advantage of life in beautiful buildings, with plentiful opportunities for recreation, exercise, and social intercourse, while the very fact of belonging to Girton or Newnham confers a certain prestige which is an advantage professionally and socially. However much we may desire the degree, and regret its indefinite postponement, it may yet safely be said that nowhere else can women obtain such advantages as at Cambridge. No anxiety need be felt about the future of the colleges. The success of their students, the influence their 'graduates' have had on the teaching profession, and the good work done by them in other fields, have amply justified the new departure. If success has come too quickly, public opinion may lag behind a few years longer. Meantime the work goes on.

At this period of their history it is no longer necessary to describe the colleges. Everybody who knows Cambridge is familiar with them. Both have increased greatly since their first beginnings. Girton has added fresh wings and a tower; changed its entrance and built a library which is full to overflowing. The trees have grown up around it and offer pleasant shade to summer tea-parties and afternoon loungers, the 'woodland walk' that encircles the grounds is gay at almost all seasons with pretty blossoms and flowering shrubs. Newnham has enlarged its first (Old) hall and built two new ones, called by names that will ever be held in honour, Clough and Sidgwick Halls. One library has been outgrown, and another—a generous gift—has been lately added; a road has been diverted allowing an addition to the grounds, and a fresh approach made under a tower gateway with beautiful iron gates presented by old students in memory of their first Principal. Girton has once more outgrown its accommodation, and is appealing for building funds. The colleges are growing both outwardly and in their aims. Not the least hopeful feature is the number of 'graduate' students who continue their studies in Cambridge or at one of the foreign universities, or devote to research or social problems that leisure and freedom from responsibility which women possess in a greater share than men. The founders have been abundantly justified in their resolve to establish no mere training-school for governesses, but to offer a wide and liberal education to all.

There are some differences in the arrangements of the two colleges. At Girton each student has two rooms, at Newnham one. The Girton fees are £105 per annum including coaching and examinations; at Newnham they are £75, but these items are not in all cases included. Girton supplies cabs for students who attend lectures in Cambridge; Newnham, being in the town, is within a walk. Both require every one who has not taken an equivalent, *e.g.* the higher certificate of the Joint Board, to pass an entrance examination. Both colleges award scholarships, though scarcely sufficient to meet the many demands from girls whose parents cannot afford the payment of full fees. Miss Welsh, one of the early Hitchin students, is now mistress of Girton; Newnham has a Vice-principal for each of the halls, and a Principal over the whole. In this post Mrs. H. Sidgwick succeeded Miss Clough, when the true foundress of Newnham died in 1892.

There is a good deal of resemblance between the Cambridge colleges and the Oxford halls, though these latter have a different history. As early as 1865 a scheme for lectures and classes at Oxford had been organised by Miss Smith, and remained in operation for several years. In 1873 another similar scheme was set on foot by a committee of ladies, with Mrs. Max Müller as treasurer, and Mrs. H. Ward and Mrs. Creighton, followed by Mrs. T. H. Green, as secretaries. The outcome of this was the Association for the Education of Women, organised in 1878, its object being 'to establish and maintain a system of instruction having general reference to the Oxford examinations.' Here as at Cambridge the next step was to found halls of residence to accommodate students from a distance. Two of these, Somerville and Lady Margaret, were opened in the same year, 1879; since then two more, St. Hugh's and St. Hilda's, have been added. The great difference, however, between the arrangements at the two Universities is that the Oxford Association, instead of amalgamating with the halls, has continued an independent existence, taking the lead in all matters concerning women's education. Most associations of this kind were temporary bodies, which dissolved when the college or school for which they were working was established, or when the particular institution with which they were connected had opened its doors to women. But the Oxford Association has increased in importance with the development of the colleges, and has become a Board of Studies for their students, and a means of communication between them and the University. One of its functions is to organise lectures, to which members of the University not infrequently request and obtain admission. It also undertakes the negotiations with the various professors and colleges that admit women to lectures, and it is thanks to its exertions that they may now attend under certain regulations lectures at almost every college in Oxford. Similarly their admission to university examinations is the work of the Association. In fact, it acts almost as a feminine department of the University, since it has to sanction the establishment of halls, make itself responsible for the studies and discipline of its students, and generally establish their connection with the University. This connection received its formal acknowledgment in 1893, when the Dean of Christchurch was appointed to represent the Hebdomadal Council on the Council of the Association, and a room in the Clarendon Building was lent it as an office.

There are some other technical differences between the position of women at Oxford and Cambridge. The latter directly acknowledges the women's colleges, the former in theory knows nothing of its women students, but leaves the Delegacy for Local Examinations to arrange for their examination. The delegates are allowed for this purpose to use the papers set by the University examiners for men, and, of course, the examinations are conducted simultaneously and under exactly the same conditions. Women may enter for every examination—whether Pass or Honours—leading to the B.A. degree, and it is this Delegacy which lays down the special conditions. In all cases a Preliminary examination is compulsory and in some an Intermediate, but neither the Delegacy nor the University demands that they should conform to the regulations imposed on men in regard to duration of study, preliminary examinations and residence. This has led to greater freedom in work; but, as often happens, this greater liberty has proved somewhat detrimental. It was difficult to gauge the value of work done under such conditions, since some students would end a four years' course with Moderations and others at once begin working for the Final Schools. Then there were some special examinations for women, which by that very restriction failed to win even the prestige they deserved, and an impression, not quite unfounded, spread abroad, of a certain vagueness in the Oxford work, which lessened its value in the eyes of the general public. There was no real gain in making a selection from a course that had been carefully planned out by the University for its members, and as this anomalous state of things had really been brought about by the gradual opening of the examinations, which made the regular course at first inaccessible to women students, there seemed no reason for continuing it when once this difficulty was removed. Oxford women got less credit often than was their due, simply because some little preliminary formality had been omitted.

In order to remedy this, and put the whole work on a firmer basis, the Association decided to institute a system of diplomas for those of its students who have taken the full course required of members of the University. This certificate is awarded only to students who have entered their names on the register qualifying for it, have kept their residence after date of entry, and passed the examinations of the B.A. course in the order and under the conditions as to standing prescribed for members of the University. Another diploma is also offered to those who have passed a course of three examinations approved by the council. Though equivalent to the B.A. diploma as regards difficulty of attainment, there appears to be little demand among recent students for this alternative course; and it will probably be regarded as a survival from the days when, the University examinations being only partially open to women, substitutes had in some cases to be devised. Certificates are also awarded to those students who have resided not less than eight terms, and have obtained a class in an Honour Examination of the University or of the Delegates of Local Examinations. These diplomas and certificates offer a definite incentive to regular study, and serve at once to show the value of the work done in each case.

At Oxford, as at Cambridge, an attempt has been made to win complete acknowledgment for women students by the conferment of the degree. An appeal was made to the University in 1895. The question came to the vote in 1896, and here, as afterwards at Cambridge, the proposal was thrown out by a considerable majority. Oxford women, like their sisters at Cambridge, must therefore wait a while longer for complete recognition. The attempt here may have been a little premature, since, owing to the late opening of the examinations and the latitude allowed to students, there were at that time very few who had fulfilled all the necessary conditions. Still the reason of the refusal was probably identical in both cases, and indicated a deep-rooted prejudice that must be overcome before further steps can be taken. Meantime the institution of the degree-certificate is giving fresh impetus to the work, and attracting larger numbers to the colleges.

Of these Somerville and Lady Margaret were founded almost simultaneously, but with somewhat different aims, the former being undenominational, the latter distinctly Church of England. Both were intended as halls of residence for Association students, but in 1881 Somerville was incorporated as a college 'to provide for the residence of women students' as well as 'for the instruction of women students and for the delivery of lectures to such students'; it was not, however, till 1894 that the term 'college' came into general use. Like the Cambridge colleges it has grown from small beginnings; it has been enlarged four times, not on one plan but by the addition of fresh buildings, so that it does not present the appearance of a connected whole. But standing in pleasant grounds among fine old trees, this very medley gives it a certain charm. It can now accommodate over seventy students, besides the Principal, secretary, and four resident tutors. Many of its old students have gained honourable positions for themselves; indeed the Principals of two leading women's colleges, Holloway and Bedford, were chosen from the ranks of old Somerville students.

Lady Margaret was founded by the Bishop of Rochester and others, and has adhered to its original plan of supplying residence to Church members of the Association. It undertakes no part of the instruction, but makes use of the Association's tutorial and lecturing staff. For some years the numbers continued small, but as they gradually increased it became necessary to construct an additional hall.

Part of this, the Wordsworth building, was occupied in 1896, when the numbers went up to forty-nine, and the council are now appealing for additional funds with which to build a chapel and the central block, to contain the library and permanent dining-hall. A pretty thatched boat-house on the Cherwell is an attractive feature of the grounds, and Lady Margaret is proud of its rowing club. The Principal is Miss Wordsworth, daughter of the late Bishop of Lincoln and great-niece of the poet. The hall takes its name from Lady Margaret Beaufort, that renowned patroness of learning, and there is a cast from her effigy in the tiny college chapel.

In close connection with Lady Margaret is St. Hugh's. It was founded in 1886 by Miss Wordsworth to provide a more economical residence for women students. By a system of sharing bedrooms and using common sitting-rooms, somewhat lower fees became practicable for those who could not afford the ordinary terms. The plan does not seem to have proved very successful, and St. Hugh's has developed into a small independent hall for twenty-five students, on the same lines as Lady Margaret, but with a graduated system of fees according to the room occupied. Like Lady Margaret it is conducted according to the principles of the Church of England, with liberty for other denominations. It also uses the tutorial staff of the Association. All students are expected to read for some University examination unless specially exempted by the Council. The Principal is Miss Moberly, daughter of the late Bishop of Salisbury.

The youngest of the Oxford halls is St. Hilda's. It was founded by Miss Beale in 1893, and meant in the first instance for students passing on from Cheltenham to Oxford. This exclusive character has, however, been abandoned, and it is now formally recognised under the rules of the Association for the Education of Women. It still receives the greater part of its students from Cheltenham, though there is nothing now to exclude others. As yet the numbers are very small. The Principal is Mrs. Burrows.

Of these four institutions, Somerville, the largest and most distinguished, is the only undenominational one. All four have the combined bedroom-studies, with common dining-halls, libraries, etc. Out-door games, debating societies, college clubs, etc. are as popular as at Cambridge. All the colleges require an entrance examination or an alternative, and all give scholarships according to ability. The fees at Somerville (including board, lodging, tuition and lectures) range from £78 to £90 according to the room occupied. At Lady Margaret they are £75, exclusive of tuition, which involves another £20 or £25. At St. Hugh's the inclusive terms range from £70 to £90; at St. Hilda's as at Lady Margaret, there is a charge of £75, which does not include tuition.

Besides those who reside at the halls other women are frequently attracted to Oxford. For these, too, the Association makes provision. Those who avail themselves of the lectures and direction of the Association, but do not reside in a hall, are registered as home students, and are placed under the care of a Principal and a committee of the Council of the Association. They are required to reside, with the Principal's approval, in a house sanctioned by the committee, and to conform to certain rules corresponding to those laid down for hall students. The Principal performs some of the functions of a tutor. Students call upon her at the beginning and end of each term, and submit to her their lists of lectures before sending them in to the office. The home students are doubtless able to pursue their studies more economically. The tuition fees seldom exceed £25, and board and lodging may be had for 25s. a week and upwards. As Oxford terms rarely exceed eight weeks it is possible by very careful management to keep expenses down to £50 to £60. As a matter of fact a large proportion of these students are daughters of Oxford residents. The arrangement is also a convenient one for foreigners who come to Oxford for a short time only. Many come in this way from America, after taking a degree in one of their own colleges. French, German, Russian, Roumanian, Danish, Swedish, and Norwegian students have at different times resided in Oxford, working at English language and literature, for the teaching diplomas of their own country. By helping these the Association can considerably increase its sphere of usefulness, and without disturbing the work of the halls it introduces a wider outlook into the lives of the students. At the same time it is open to home students to take the regular course, and several of them do so. The committee only registers those who take up a systematic course of study, extending over at least three terms, but even those who come for a shorter time can attend its lectures and profit by its help.

By these varied means the Association is able to draw together all the agencies for women's education at Oxford; in 1897 the number of students on its books was 202, and there is every reason to expect a considerable increase now that the institution of the degree-diploma has given a fresh impulse to the work. The steady flow from our girls' schools to both Universities proves that the colleges have won appreciation through the whole of the country. Happily many of the founders are yet among us to enjoy the fruits of the labours. Girton and Newnham, Somerville and Lady Margaret, bear eloquent testimony to the truth that the dreamers of visions are often those who see furthest and best.

CHAPTER VII

ADMISSION TO UNIVERSITIES

THE position of women at Oxford and Cambridge is so anomalous as to require a good deal of explanation, and indeed it is sometimes said that the only real grievance these students have is the difficulty of making people understand what they may and what they may not do. There is no such difficulty when we come to the newer universities. Here the course has been one of steady progress, and one after another all the barriers have fallen.

London was the pioneer in this reform, and its exceptional position made it an excellent field for experiment. A mere examining and degree-conferring body, the London University was not obliged to face those difficult questions of residence, teaching, and discipline which had to be considered elsewhere. It was natural that women who desired to obtain professional qualifications without being compelled to seek them outside their own country, should apply to London for help. As early as 1856 Miss J. M. White had addressed a letter to the Registrar, inquiring whether a woman could become a candidate for a diploma in medicine. Counsel's opinion was taken in the matter and proved adverse. In 1872 it was again raised by Miss Elizabeth Garrett (now Mrs. Garrett Anderson) who requested admission as a candidate for matriculation. She was refused on the same ground. Since it appeared that the University had not power to accede to these requests, a memorial was drawn up begging it to seek for such modifications in its charter as would enable it to admit women to examination. The motion was brought before the Senate, and lost by the casting vote of the Chancellor. With success so nearly attained the advocates of the change determined not to let the matter drop, and after a while a modified proposal was made. It was thought that a special examination for women might meet the case, or at any rate serve as an experiment in what was then a very new field. The first was held in May 1869, and followed the lines of Matriculation with some modifications. As an isolated examination of no special difficulty and leading nowhere, it did not attract large numbers, and it became more and more clear that what women needed was not so much a special course of study as—to quote the words of the Calendar—'to have access to the ordinary degrees and honours, and to be subject to the same tests of qualification which were imposed on other students.' The result of this conviction was that in 1878 it was decided to accept from the Crown 'a supplemental charter, making every degree, honour, and prize awarded by the University accessible to students of both sexes on perfectly equal terms.' The charter, however, declared that no woman should be a member of Convocation until Convocation should itself pass a resolution admitting them. In 1882, almost as soon as there was any woman eligible, this resolution was passed, and henceforth both sexes were placed on an absolute equality in their treatment by London University.

There is no need to dwell on the success of this new departure. The London degrees have been eagerly sought by women, and they have won distinguished places in the class lists. Among its graduates London numbers over fifty female M.A.'s, six D.Sc.'s, one D.Lit., to say nothing of many hundred B.A. and B.Sc., as well as all the medical degrees. Class lists show no special division into masculine and feminine studies, since women have won high honours in classics, and men in modern languages. Even on Presentation-Day special allusions to the lady-graduates are seldom made in the speeches; it is no longer considered a matter of surprise that women should hold their own intellectually. The London class lists with their rigid equality have proved to demonstration the equality of the sexes as far as concerns the domain of examination. And at the particular moment when this was done, it was the greatest service that could be rendered to the cause of women's education, since it settled once and for all the question of making special conditions for them.

But throwing open the examinations and degrees of London was only an indirect assistance to their education, since the University examines all who come, but asks no questions as to how or where they gained their teaching. There was one institution already in existence which was only waiting for this new impulse to enlarge the scope of its work. Bedford College had been gradually developing from humble beginnings into an institution of first-class educational importance. In 1874 it had been removed from Bedford Square to its present premises in York Place, Baker Street, and here it has been gradually expanding, adding another house, building on at the back, supplying now one laboratory now another, until it has reached its present condition of efficiency, taking its place as the leading women's college of London. Its success is probably due to the progressive action of its council, ever ready to realise new needs and meet each fresh demand as it arose. Recognising the transformation which the opening of the London degrees must effect in women's education, they at once proceeded to open classes in the subjects of the examinations. At the first Matriculation Examination to which women were admitted, five Bedford College students presented themselves, and all took Honours. In due course classes for B.A. work were added, then B.Sc., then M.A., and in all these Bedford College students acquitted themselves well. The college had now won an honourable place among university colleges, and in 1894 it was included among the list of those entitled to a share of the annual grant of £15,000 to university colleges in Great Britain. From this source it received £700, since increased to £1200, and it now receives also an annual grant of £500 from the London Technical Education Board, for the further equipment of the laboratories and development of practical work in science. This is a speciality of Bedford College. Its laboratories for biology, botany, chemistry, geology, physiology, and physics meet every requirement.

The college is still open to girls who attend only single courses, but the majority enter as regular students, and work either for a London degree or the alternative college course. Bedford has also added other departments of study to the ordinary curriculum. It has an art school, a training department for teachers, and a special hygiene course, for which certificates are conferred. And finally it has developed, as far as its accommodation will permit, into a residential college. The old-fashioned dormitory boarding accommodation has been abolished in favour of students' rooms in the bed-study fashion so familiar at Newnham and Oxford, and the general management has been placed in the hands of a Principal. Miss Emily Penrose, the first to fill this post, has now become Principal of Holloway, and her place is taken by Miss Ethel Hurlbatt, late Warden of Aberdare Hall.

Bedford College, true to its undenominational principles, has never introduced religious instruction into its curriculum. It is not unnatural that a wish has been expressed in some quarters for a residential college, which should prepare its students for London degrees and at the same time take cognisance of their religious training. It was for this end that Westfield College at Hampstead was founded in 1882. Its benefactor was Miss Dudin Brown, who made over to trustees the sum of £10,000 'for the establishment of a college for the higher education of women on Christian principles.' The Principal is Miss Maynard, one of the early students of Girton, who has introduced into Westfield many of the arrangements of the parent college. The two-room plan, which has found too few imitators, is the rule here. Inclusive fees, as at Girton, are £105 a year. The conditions for admission are similar. There are three entrance scholarships, open to girls who have passed the London Matriculation in Honours or in the first division.

The college began its work in hired houses at Hampstead, but building soon became necessary. It is pleasantly situated in that most attractive of the London suburbs, and combines some advantages of both town and country. Though it has no laboratories of its own, students can easily reach those of Bedford College to which they have access; and similarly it is easy to supply from London such teaching as cannot be undertaken by the resident staff. Westfield students take high places in the class lists, and it supplies an important addition to the London colleges.

In enumerating these we cannot omit Holloway, for though far beyond the borders of the metropolis, it is more and more assimilating its teaching to the London work. Such was not, however, its original purpose. Among those who attended the meeting in 1867 to consider the foundation of a women's college, was Mr. Thomas Holloway, and at one time it was hoped he would prove a benefactor to it. But Mr. Holloway preferred the idea of an independent college unconnected with a university, like Vassar and others in the United States, and his wishes were thus expressed: 'It is the founder's desire that power by Act of Parliament, Royal Charter, or otherwise, should ultimately be sought, enabling the college to confer degrees on its students after proper examination in the various subjects of instruction.' With this end in view he chose a beautiful site near Egham, and built upon it a most elaborate and fully equipped college, which should some day develop into a women's university. Nothing was spared that could contribute to the comfort and well-being of the students. Each has two rooms; and the magnificent dining-hall, museum, picture-gallery, etc. prove that no pains were spared to make the new college attractive as well as efficient. For all that, it was viewed at first with some misgivings, for it seemed to lack a definite aim. It was formally opened by the Queen in 1886, and in the following year Miss Bishop was appointed Principal, but students came in slowly. A liberal provision of scholarships, and the beauty and healthy situation of the college did much to dispel the first misgivings, especially when it began to appear from results that the teaching too was of the best. The founder had himself directed that until the power to confer degrees should have been obtained 'it is intended that the students shall qualify themselves to take the degrees at the University of London or any other university of the United Kingdom whose degrees may be obtained by them, or to pass any examination open to them at any such university, which may be equivalent to a degree examination.' In accordance with this permission the first students were prepared for the London degrees, and also for the examinations of the University of Oxford, which under present conditions are open to all comers, since the delegacy takes no cognisance of residence. Holloway students may therefore, if they please, present themselves for examination in Moderations and Final Schools just as if they were residing at the Oxford halls. They cannot, of course, obtain the Association's diploma, and miss the advantage of the Oxford lectures.

On these lines the college worked for ten years, when circumstances made it necessary to reconsider its position. At both Oxford and Cambridge the degree had been refused, and it seemed desirable for the friends of women's education to come to some decision on their future policy. Once again the scheme of a women's university was raised; and Holloway College took the lead in calling a meeting to discuss the question. Opinions were invited as to the future action of the college, and three propositions were made: (1) That Holloway College should, in accordance with the founder's will, seek powers to confer its own degrees. (2) That a Federal University should be founded, to include in its jurisdiction all the women's colleges. (3) That Holloway should associate itself more closely with London, and seek admission into its teaching University when this should be founded. The discussion showed a strong consensus in favour of this last proposal, and it is probable that henceforth the work of Holloway College will be chiefly directed towards the London courses. If so, it will be safe to predict for it a brilliant future. Its healthy situation, delightful grounds, beautiful buildings, and large endowment, with the prospect of receiving full recognition for work done, will attract large numbers; indeed with Holloway, Bedford, and Westfield for their own, London women have little left to desire. Whatever they may lack elsewhere fullest measure is dealt to them here.

Nor are they even restricted to their own special colleges. The classes at University College are open to all who care to attend; indeed this was one of the first, if not the very first, of our English colleges to try the co-education experiment. After experimenting by holding some classes for women separately, and admitting them temporarily to others, the professors decided in favour of joint classes, and the result was the opening of all except the departments of Medicine and Engineering. The results proved altogether satisfactory, and this end has been helped by the appointment of a lady-superintendent, who holds the same position towards the women students that a vice-dean does to the men. No woman is admitted as a student except upon her recommendation, and upon production of satisfactory references. In this way their special interests are safeguarded, and girls far from home may always secure friendly advice and guidance. Further, there is a special residence provided at College Hall, Byng Place, where students may have some of the advantages of college life while pursuing their studies at University College, or the Woman's Medical School close by. With Miss Grove as Principal, and Miss Morison, superintendent of the women students, as Vice-Principal, it offers a bright and cultivated home to its inmates, and keeps up the collegiate idea by admitting only such as have already passed Matriculation or an equivalent examination, and are pursuing a regular course of study. The fees for board and residence vary, according to the room occupied and the length of the term, from £51 to £90 the session.

To give a complete list of the institutions that prepare students for the London degrees, would be impossible, since it is open to any person in any place to hold such classes. A few work for them at the ladies' department of King's College, but on the whole the work of this branch is more on the lines of miscellaneous lectures and general culture. Some schools, *e.g.* the North London and the Bedford High School, also carry on their pupils beyond Matriculation to the Intermediate examinations, or even further. The Ladies' College, Cheltenham, provides instruction for the full Arts course. Most of the provincial university colleges have London degree classes, and many candidates, who cannot get oral teaching, make use of the University Tutorial and other correspondence classes.

A new development on fresh lines is supplied by the Polytechnics. In most of these, whether in London or other large towns, classes are held in all the subjects of the London examinations with particular assistance for Science. With fully equipped laboratories, a large staff of teachers, and considerable funds at their disposal, the Polytechnics may yet become formidable rivals to the other London colleges. Some regret this new departure, and believe that such institutions would be better employed in confining themselves to their original function, the encouragement of handicraft; on the other hand, a system of cheap local colleges is so valuable to large numbers that it is not likely to be abandoned. Some place must be found in the new organisation of the London University for these institutes, if they themselves desire it; but perhaps we shall see, instead of this, a federation of these great science and handicraft schools into some fresh University of their own.

The example set by London in 1879 was soon to be imitated. Only a year afterwards a new University was founded, and the principle of including women was at once adopted. The charter of Victoria University distinctly stated that its degrees and distinctions might be conferred 'on all persons, male or female, who shall have pursued a regular course of study in a College in the University, and shall submit themselves for examination.' The degree is somewhat on the lines of the London, but attendance at certain prescribed courses of study is required. These courses must be continued for three years at least. Hence admission to the Victoria degrees really depends on the action of the individual colleges, which are quite unfettered by the University. These are—(1) Owens College, Manchester; (2)

University College, Liverpool; (3) Yorkshire College, Leeds.

The first of these had been in existence as a men's college some years before the establishment of the University, and it has not seemed anxious to make changes in its original constitution. It became necessary to organise a special department for women, in connection with which they still receive some of their instruction. But the teaching for the higher examinations, *i.e.* those beyond the Victoria Preliminary, is received in the ordinary college classes. As a matter of fact, men and women are taught together in nearly all the B.A. and B.Sc. classes; and the Preliminary, like the London Matriculation, belongs to school work, and has no proper place in a college curriculum at all. Owens still follows the old plan, now almost everywhere discarded, of offering special certificates to women on easier terms; but for these there is little demand.

Since University College, Liverpool was not incorporated till 1881, *i.e.* after the constitution of the University, it was natural that it should follow its lead in the recognition of women, but this was not yet full and ungrudging. The charter says: 'female students may be admitted to attend any of the courses of instruction established in the college, subject to such restrictions and regulations as statutes of the College may from time to time prescribe.' At present the regulations stand thus: 'Female students may be admitted to the classes of the College, except those of the Medical School, under regulations to be framed by the Senate and approved by the Council.' In theory, therefore, University is a men's college that admits women. In fact, with the exception of the medical classes, the two are pretty much on an equality. Men and women are admitted on the same terms to the day and evening classes; throughout the regulations the words 'his or her' are used. Rules apply to both sexes alike. Hitherto the college has been of use chiefly to Liverpool residents, and for such it was doubtless intended, but it is just about to extend the sphere of its usefulness by opening a Hall of Residence for Women. The fees for residence are to be £40 to £55 per annum. College tuition fees are about £20 to £25. The total expenses would therefore be a little less than at Newnham. Liverpool can hardly offer the attractions of Cambridge, but the hall should prove useful for girls in the North who do not wish to go too far from home, or to whom the right to use the degree letters is of some special value. And since Cambridge and Oxford can by no means attempt to accommodate the whole of the ever-increasing contingent of women students, it is well that there should be many and varied opportunities of study offered them elsewhere.

At the Yorkshire College, Leeds, all the classes are open to women as to men, and all have been attended by them except the purely professional ones and the medical school. This college chiefly supplies local needs, as far, at any rate, as girls are concerned; for its specialities, such as coal-mining, dyeing, leather, and textile industries, etc. naturally do not appeal to women. It is to a great extent a technological college, receiving assistance from the Clothworkers', Skinners', and other city companies. But it has also an Arts department, where students can be prepared for Victoria or London examinations, and this is of great use to boys and girls who pass on from their respective schools.

The last of the English Universities to admit women was Durham. As compared with Oxford and Cambridge, it is a recent foundation, since it received its charter in 1837. Since one of its most important faculties is Divinity, it seemed a less suitable field than others for feminine study, but a change was effected by the foundation, in 1871, of the Newcastle College of Science, in connection with Durham, which admitted students of both sexes to scientific and medical classes. It then became important to win the University hall-mark for the women, and after a while Durham was induced to apply for the necessary powers. In 1895 it received a supplementary charter, giving power to confer degrees on women in all faculties except divinity. With this exception, women are admitted as members of the University on the same terms as men. All lectures are open to them. Male students reside for the most part in college as at Oxford and Cambridge; the women studying at Durham are therefore at present unattached members. This state of things will be remedied as soon as a regular women's college is opened at Durham; special scholarships for women are already offered, to attract larger numbers. At Newcastle, which at present receives the majority of the women students, a hostel has been opened for them. The number of lady graduates is as yet of necessity small.

It is significant of the steady advance of public opinion on the subject of women's education, that the youngest of all our universities is the one to do them fullest justice. It is the proud boast of the University of Wales that its charter contains the following clause: 'Women shall be eligible equally with men for admittance to any degree, which the University is, by this our Charter, authorised to confer. Every office hereby created in the University, and the membership of every authority hereby constituted, shall be open to women equally with men.'

The University of Wales is a federation of three constituent colleges, all much older than the University itself, and they in their turn represent aspirations which the fable-loving Cymry trace back to hoary days of antiquity. Caerleon-on-Usk, they tell us, was the precursor of the present *Prifysgol Cymru*; and when in the ninth century Alfred the Great determined to found the comparatively modern University of Oxford, it was to Wales he sent for professors. When, in 1893, the royal seal was set to the charter of the Welsh University, it symbolised the revival of ancient and departed glories.

However little faith we may attach to some of these tales, one thing is certain. The aspirations which expressed themselves in the foundation of Aberystwyth College had dwelt among the people for many generations. At last, in the early fifties, it was resolved to found a University College for Wales, but the problem whence to obtain the funds was not easy to solve. Appeal was made for voluntary contributions, and they came, some large, some small, all giving according to their means. Still it was not till twenty years after the first suggestion that the college came into being. In 1872, when Aberystwyth was opened, Girton had already made its first start at Hitchin, and the house of residence, that was to develop into Newnham, had been opened at Cambridge; but these beginnings were too small to attract general attention, and the new college became, as a matter of course, an institution for male students only. There was nothing to forbid the admission of women, it was simply a thing no one had contemplated; and when, at last, in 1883, a few women students did present themselves, no one thought of shutting the door on them. When the college charter was conferred in 1889, it simply recognised the fact of their presence by the clause: 'Female students shall be admitted to all the benefits and emoluments of the College, and women shall be eligible to sit on the Governing body, on the Council, and on the Senate.'

Prosperity did not come all at once to Aberystwyth. It had at first to struggle against two great evils: lack of funds, and the insufficient preliminary training of its students. Appeal was made for Government help in both directions, and the result of frequent representations was the appointment, by the Lord President of the Council, of a departmental committee, to inquire into the whole state of Welsh education. In 1881 this committee reported that a case had been made out for Government aid to both secondary and higher education in Wales, and recommended the establishment of two colleges, one in North and one in South Wales, and the eventual foundation of a Welsh University. A grant of £2500, afterwards increased to £4000, was at once made to Aberystwyth; in 1883 the South Wales College was founded at Cardiff, and in the following year the Northern College was begun at Bangor, each receiving an annual grant of £4000. Both, from the first, opened their doors to women.

For the first ten years the colleges directed their courses of study towards the degrees of the University of London. Their students did well, but the desire for their own University and their own degrees never faded from the minds of Welshmen. A few eager spirits met again and again in conference, then followed meetings of educationalists all over the principality, and in 1891 the main lines of a university were laid down by public conference, details were discussed by a representative committee, referred back to the conference, then to the colleges, and the sixteen Welsh county councils; lastly, the press and the general public were called upon for an opinion, and then the scheme was laid before the President of the Council. If ever there was a national University, the Welsh may claim to have established one. In November 1893 the royal seal was affixed to the charter, and in June 1895 the University held its first Matriculation Examination.

The degree course of the University of Wales is a complicated one, and is by no means planned so that he who runs may read. It has a twofold, or rather a threefold aim. The University not only takes cognisance of residence, but also lays down very careful directions as to the manner in which students shall obtain their knowledge. Not only does it demand a three years' course in a constituent college of the University, but it also prescribes the nature of the courses, and the number of lectures to be attended. After Matriculation, which must be passed in five subjects, three compulsory, and two optional, and may be taken in one year or in two, the regulations require each student to pursue not less than ten courses, of which one must be in elementary Logic, and one, at least, a course of Latin or Greek. Apart from the Logic, the nine courses must be chosen in not less than three, or more than six departments. The possible courses are designated according to their degree of difficulty, as intermediate, ordinary, and special; four, at least, must be of higher grade than intermediate. In order to distribute them evenly over the whole term of residence, no candidate may take more than four in any one year, or more than seven in the first two years. A course is held to include not less than eighty lectures, and the corresponding examination; and since, in most subjects, the intermediate course must be pursued before the higher ones are attempted, every student has to attend some very elementary lectures before proceeding to anything at all like university work. As sixteen is the college age of admission, this arrangement is probably intentional; the colleges are meant to continue school work for one year at least, and gradually lead the student on to more arduous labours.

Since the colleges are independent institutions, they have a good deal of freedom in the organisation of their work, and may, if they please, submit new schemes for the consideration of the Senate, the other two colleges, and the University Court. Without the sanction of all these they cannot attempt any innovation. The superior stress laid on the actual instruction rather than on the ensuing examination is emphasised by appointing the three professors of each subject as examiners, with the help of one outside person, who must be some one of distinguished attainments and authority.

Thus the University of Wales proceeds on lines which, though new to us, bear considerable resemblance to the plan of many American colleges, where the number of hours to be spent weekly in the lecture-room counts as part qualification for the degree, and the examinations are spread out over the whole term of residence, and not concentrated into one or two supreme efforts. Of course this greatly relieves the strain, and it is too soon to say whether the degree will at all lose in prestige from the numerous efforts made to clear the student's path of thorns. It is probably the best system for Wales, where the Intermediate schools only profess to keep their pupils till seventeen, and there is nothing to prevent able students from competing for scholarships, which shall enable them to continue at Oxford or Cambridge the studies begun in one of their own colleges. Eventually it is probable that facilities will be offered for doing advanced work without forsaking their own country.

Even before the establishment of the University, the colleges attracted many women students from England as well as Wales. All three are pleasantly situated in healthy spots, and the cheapness of both teaching and living helped to attract many girls. It thus soon became necessary to consider the question of a mixed university, which had no residential colleges to simplify the problem. Soon it became clear that, where young people of both sexes were very frequently thrown together, it was desirable in the interests of all concerned to exercise some sort of control. A hall of residence for the women seemed the best way out of the dilemma, and it had the advantage of drawing them away from lonely and often uncomfortable lodgings, and giving them some of that feeling of corporate life which is valued so highly at the older universities. Still it is noteworthy that, to make the plan a success, residence has had, under certain conditions, to be made compulsory. The first attempt at Aberystwyth was a failure, but in 1887 another house was taken, and compulsory residence required. This arrangement seemed to attract students; in the following session their numbers increased, and continued to average about forty, till in 1891 it was resolved to build a large new hall. The numbers then again went up, and have already reached 175. Alexandra Hall was opened with much state by the Princess of Wales in June 1897. It can accommodate 200, a number which must soon be reached.

Neither Bangor nor Cardiff can boast such numbers, but in both the hostels are doing well. At Bangor, after a few years' experiment, it was decided to make residence compulsory for all girls under twenty-one. The hall and college were brought into close connection by the appointment of a lady, who was also an officer of the college, to act as superintendent of all the women students. Permission is given to women to reside in any house which, in the judgment of the Principal and Lady-superintendent, provides hostel conditions of supervision. At Aberdare Hall, Cardiff, there is compulsory residence for women who do not live in their own homes. At all three halls the fees are very low, forty guineas being the usual annual payment for board and residence, and £10 for the composition tuition charge. At Bangor and Cardiff there are also a few cubicles, for which the charge is only thirty guineas. This plan hardly appears to answer, nor does it seem desirable to let the standard of comfort fall below a certain minimum. There is a talk of abandoning it.

In estimating the numbers at these colleges, we must remember that they do not represent only students in Arts and Science. All three have established day training-departments, and to these students, too, the halls are open, as well as to those who attend the Cardiff Cookery School. In attempting to put the training for domestic economy and elementary school teaching on the same footing as university work, Wales is acting in accordance with its democratic traditions, and trying also to induce a higher class of students to take up the elementary teaching. The experiment is certainly worth making, and it will be interesting to watch its success. English high school girls who wish to take up elementary teaching might here combine their training and their work for the Welsh degree in a three years' course.

With the help of the wardens of halls and the ladies' committees, the colleges are able to face the complications of joint clubs and societies for both sexes. All these involve some special regulations, in regard to the composition of committees, the return from evening meetings, etc. but the difficulties have not proved insuperable. It would hardly be going too far to say that the women's halls of residence have saved the situation in Wales, and made this most complete example of co-education possible. It is not surprising that they are being adopted elsewhere. The advocates of educational equality for the sexes, even where the instruction is given to both together, have assuredly no desire to complicate or revolutionise social relations, nor yet to confer full liberty on those who are hardly emerged from the schoolgirl stage. For both sexes the residential arrangement seems on many grounds desirable, and while congratulating the women on their pleasant halls of residence, we can but hope that the male students may not be left out in the cold much longer, without the chance of learning for themselves the true meaning of collegiate life.

The opportunities for advanced study open to women have indeed increased and multiplied at a rapid rate during the last few years. Beyond the northern boundary we find all the Scottish Universities have admitted them freely to membership, and if we cross St. George's Channel, the Royal University of Ireland—like London, only an examining body—takes no note of sex, and even Trinity College, Dublin, is making some tentative essays in the teaching and examining of women. This represents what has been done in our own islands, but the same movement has been going on simultaneously all over the world. Thanks to Mr. M. E. Sadler,[15] we are now in a position to compare the position of women at a hundred and thirty-nine different Universities. Questions were sent to the Universities of Great Britain and Ireland, the continent of Europe, the United States of America, Canada, India, and Australia. 'It appears,' says Mr. Sadler, 'that at a hundred of these, the distinctions between men and women students are, if any, comparatively unimportant; at seven Universities women students are admitted, by courtesy or special permission, to some lectures and examinations; at twenty-one others women are, by like favour, admitted to some of the lectures; and at eleven Universities they are not admitted at all.' Of the exceptions five are in Germany, three in Russia, one in Ireland, one in Belgium, one in the United States. France and Italy are specially remarkable for their generous recognition of women, and Germany, long obdurate, is making constant fresh concessions; but intending students should study the special conditions of the one they wish to attend, since many of the regulations are most complicated.[16]

This general advance all over the civilised world is the chief gain this half century has brought to women's education. Though each country has proceeded on its own lines the movement has unconsciously been an international one. That gives it a strength which will make it permanent.

[15] *Special Reports on Educational Subjects,* 1896–97.

[16] See *Handbook to Courses Open to Women in British, Continental, and Canadian Universities,* by Isabel Maddison, B.Sc., Ph.D.

CHAPTER VIII

BOARDING AND PRIVATE SCHOOLS

Once more our chronicle takes us back to 1867. A new era was then inaugurated, that of girls' day schools. Not that these were anything new; small cheap day-schools for girls abounded, but the majority of them were bad. With fees ranging from £3 to £10 a year, and pupils of every variety of age, a little simple arithmetic will prove that the mistress had not sufficient funds at her disposal to pay for suitable premises and adequate teaching, to say nothing of winning a modest competence for herself. From all parts of the country came condemnation of these small, cheap schools. The opinions about boarding-schools were by no means so unanimous. They were censured for the excessive attention given to accomplishments, the insufficient education of the teachers, and their neglect of physical training; but these were faults common to nearly all the schools of that day, and not characteristic of boarding-schools as such. A careful perusal of the Commissioners' report leads to a far more favourable impression of boarding than day-schools, due, probably, to their being less hampered for funds. But the general public is influenced by impressions rather than facts; and certainly an impression did gain ground that a day-school was in itself a good and a boarding-school an evil.

Unquestionably the reformers were right in first turning their attention to the former. Large schools of this kind were easier to organise, and really made for efficiency and economy, that much desired combination, which in this case is not, as so often, a mere contradiction in terms. The establishment of high and endowed schools has brought a good education within reach of thousands of girls who could by no other means have obtained it. The extinction of the small, cheap boarding-school which for the past century had been struggling to give the lower middle classes a poorer imitation of the poor education given elsewhere to their social 'superiors,' is a thing no one can seriously deplore. Painless extinction is, unhappily, impossible. The suffering which such changes bring in their train is to be deplored, but the article itself may be relegated to the class of those that 'never will be missed.'

The new day-schools met a real want, and success came to them at once. It was natural they should attract the first relays of the 'graduates' that the women's colleges were beginning to send out. Thus they were the first to introduce improved teaching, and for a while they were supposed to have a monopoly of it. In the prevailing dearth of good mistresses they were able to get first choice; now, after the lapse of thirty years, the supply exceeds the demand, and a good teacher is attainable by any school of any grade that can satisfy the very moderate demands of university women.

The high schools started with a very definite principle—the combination of school teaching with home influence—doubtless the ideal for all girls, supposing that each side duly fulfils its share of the obligation. But now, in 1898, it is curious to note how far the high school has travelled in twenty-five years. The original scheme of morning-school, from nine to one, and afternoon preparation for a few girls who had no quiet room at home, still prevails in theory, but *quantum mutatus ab illo* can best be realised by tracing a day's routine in school. First come the morning lessons, usually five in number, with the short break for play or drill, then the school dinner, to which over fifty girls sometimes sit down; again a short interval before the afternoon classes, music lessons and preparation, which usually go on till four, though girls who have no special duties at the time may be found at play in the playground. Still later, if it be summer, there may be an adjournment to the school field, often at a considerable distance. Not till darkness sets in can it be said that the day's school life is over; and the elder girls still have some lessons to prepare before bed-time. A healthful, well-filled happy day is behind them, but where does the home influence come in? The girls might as well be weekly boarders for all the share they have in the real life of home. Saturday may see a cricket practice or a work party, or a school committee, or a sketching expedition, or a match with some distant school. Sunday alone belongs to the home. The numerous clubs, charities, old girls' meetings, etc. fill up all the time the girls can spare from their lessons. Girls who do not live quite near frequently become day-boarders, though the word is not used, and take dinner, and sometimes even tea, at school. In some few cases the school even undertakes to supply medical supervision and the general direction of the pupil's health, thus relieving parents of one more responsibility. In fact the day-school is well on the road to become a boarding-school, and the establishment of boarding-houses more or less loosely connected with it is a further step in the same direction.

How far these schools have travelled from their original intentions becomes evident if we refer back to a controversy on school hours that took place in 1880 in consequence of some strictures passed by Mrs. Garrett Anderson on the arrangements in the High Schools. She considered the strain of the four hours' morning excessive, and proposed reducing it, introducing afternoon school and a considerable interval for outdoor games between the two. This was met with general opposition by headmistresses. Day-schools, it was said, could not be expected to provide dinner, it was most undesirable for girls to return from school as late as four or five on cold winter afternoons, teachers could not be expected to undertake so much afternoon work, while the strongest opposition of all was made to the games. Miss Buss pointed out that the mixture of classes which was unobjectionable as long as girls only met at lessons where talking was forbidden, or in the short intervals which were largely devoted to lunch and drill, might cause serious difficulties if the whole day were spent in school. She also thought the games would be a difficulty; only rough girls would take part in them, and the rest simply lounge about.

How wrong these predictions have proved we all know. Girls' athletics have made startling progress during the last ten years; cricket and hockey, seemingly rough games, have found favour with the most feminine of girls; the school dinner is a regular institution, and is accompanied by pleasant chat about practices, matches, election of club officers, etc. A new feature, never contemplated by the promoters, has entered these day-schools; and, oddly enough, is doing more than anything else to bring back to favour the once despised boarding-school.

Those that now originated were of a new kind, at least for girls; schools where the boarding-houses form part of the regular organisation, and the whole life and development of the girls is under the charge of the mistresses. Something of the sort had already been done at Cheltenham, and doubtless the College owed much of its success to its boarding-house system. Although a general English education, which is wanted by all alike, can be supplied in any town capable of supporting a large day-school, the very special teaching wanted by a few girls working for scholarships or specially advanced examinations causes a severe strain on the resources of a moderate-sized school, is impossible for financial reasons in a small one, and quite inaccessible to those girls with country homes from whom a considerable proportion of college students is drawn. Hence there arose a new type of school.

The first of this kind originated in Scotland, at St. Andrews. It was founded in 1877 by a local company with a view to educating their own daughters; but arrangements were at once made for taking boarders, and these were placed under the immediate charge of the head-mistress. As the numbers increased, other houses were taken and placed under charge of senior mistresses; and as more and more girls were attracted from a distance, the boarding element began to predominate. With Miss Lumsden, one of the 'Girton pioneers,' as first head-mistress, and Miss Dove, another student of Hitchin days, as her successor, the school very quickly settled down into lines very closely resembling those of a boys' public school. The boarding-houses became an integral part of the institution, the school-house being under the charge of the head-mistress, and the others under the senior assistants. In this way the staff of the school was strengthened by the encouragement thus offered to women of ability to remain in the school instead of seeking their promotion elsewhere. The boarding-houses are also valuable in ensuring regular attendance and proper home preparation, since the day-girls, being in a minority, cannot introduce those lax ideas of attendance which are in some places unfortunately the result of the much vaunted home influence.

The numbers in the school are limited to 200. The admission age is thirteen or fourteen, no girl can be admitted who has turned seventeen. All must pass an entrance examination, graduated according to age, but always including a certain amount of Arithmetic, English, Latin and French. A school of 200 girls, all between thirteen and nineteen, and all with a sufficient preparatory training, can genuinely concentrate its efforts on higher teaching. The classes become easier to group, and with a large staff which allows of careful subdividing, all the ordinary hindrances to progress are removed, and a school is enabled to work under the best possible conditions. It can, if it is desired, make a speciality of certain branches of study. At St. Andrews classics take an important place; of the present staff five have passed the Classical Tripos. Among the honours won by old pupils are first classes in Classical Moderations and Final Classical Schools at Oxford, and in the Classical Tripos at Cambridge. The school distinctly aims at a literary curriculum, with the higher certificate of the Joint Board to fix the standard, and Oxford or Cambridge as the goal for those girls whose education is to be continued.

St. Leonard's School, as it has been called since it acquired the old buildings and beautiful grounds of the ancient St. Leonard's College, is organised with a school-house and seven boarding-houses, each under the charge of a mistress. With all the girls under the control of the head-mistress it is possible to carry out the prefect system, and, by giving a good deal of responsibility to the Sixth Form, remove that element of excessive supervision which was often a harmful element in the old-fashioned boarding-school. Each house constitutes a small community, with its separate dining-room and study, where each of the elder girls has a small writing-table and bookshelf. Some rules prevail in all, *e.g.* that no work shall be done before breakfast or after 8.30 P.M. School hours are from 9 to 12.30 every day, with special subjects in the afternoon. After dinner about one and a half hours are given to games under charge of a special mistress. There is a playground of sixteen acres, which comprises cricket-field, golf-course, lawn and gravel tennis-courts, large hockey-courts and fives-courts, etc. The St. Leonard's girls are renowned for their skill in games.

With a school thus organised the life of the girls is made easier. There is no conflict of aims; in term-time the school claims its due, in holidays the home. Whether this is theoretically the best plan is an academic rather than a practical question, but it is undoubtedly beneficial to the studies and health of the girls. A mistress who is intimately acquainted with the work of every Form can check overwork more effectually than the most anxious mother, who is incapable of judging from that school point of view which looms so large in the young girl's mind. Loyalty and public spirit, developed by this joint life of small communities within a large one, are important factors in forming character, and the general atmosphere of alternate work and play without the excessive excitement of home gaieties and the distraction of domestic interests unquestionably facilitates study. Whether the gains to character really outweigh the advantages of the family life depends so entirely on the arrangements and atmosphere of each particular home, that it is impossible to give any general opinion. At any rate results seem to show that this class of school is one of the chief needs for girls at the present time. A good deal of attention had been drawn to St. Leonard's School in England, and in spite of the distance many girls were in the habit of journeying northwards three times a year for the sake of sharing in its advantages. At last a number of educationalists decided to establish a school of this kind in England, and induced Miss Dove, who had now placed the Northern school on a thoroughly satisfactory basis, to organise a similar one in the South. The Education Company, Limited, was formed, with a council of which the Master of Trinity became president. It was fortunate enough to secure for its first school the beautiful house and grounds of Wycombe Abbey. Situated in lovely country, with thirty-six acres of its own, and the rest of the park stretched all about it, the old trees, the historic memories and dignified surroundings help to shed over the school some of that feeling of tradition and veneration for the past, which all girls' institutions must of themselves lack for some time to come.

The school resembles St. Leonard's in its organisation, with some slight differences. There are no day pupils and, as the Abbey is itself capable of accommodating a hundred girls, it is divided for school purposes into four divisions, technically known as 'houses.' Each house is in the special charge of its tutor, and has its own sitting-room and dormitories, and its table in the dining-room. The house-colour is carried out in the cubicles; cretonnes, bed-spreads, tiles, etc. being red, blue, green, or yellow, according to the special house in which the dormitory is situated. All this prettiness serves as an attractive background for hard work and healthy play. It is pleasant to find the modern school catering for all the sides of a girl's nature.

It very soon became necessary to build, and with the help of the new houses two hundred can now be accommodated. Beyond this it is not proposed to go; but should the system prove as popular in England as in Scotland, it is probable that the Education Company might open more schools. The conditions of admission, entrance examination, etc. are the same as at St. Andrews. Physical exercise plays an important part, and about two hours every day are given up to games or country walks, which groups of girls are allowed to take together. Each term has its own special game; lacrosse is the favourite in the autumn, hockey in winter, and cricket in summer. The heavy work of the day is thus broken up into two parts, and Wycombe, unlike the majority of girls' schools, does not rigidly divide these into morning classes, afternoon preparation. Lessons and study hours alternate during the day. This is an attempt to relieve the strain of the long morning, against which many voices are again being raised. Physical and manual training come in for a share of attention, two hours a day in the upper, and three in the lower school. Under these headings come drawing and painting, part-singing, practising, dancing, gymnastics, carpentry, gardening, and needlework. All these are taught by expert teachers, and are treated as an integral part of the general education. In the upper forms six hours a day are given to actual study, in the lower only five. As this includes preparation, and the day is so fully occupied that there is not much chance of stealing odd half hours for work, it will be interesting to see whether this short allowance, with the help of careful arrangement and healthful surroundings, will prove sufficient to prepare girls adequately for college. It is too soon to ask for results, but if this plan succeeds, a problem which engages much attention at present will have been greatly helped towards solution.

Another school that is doing useful work, as what our American cousins would call an 'experiment station,' is the one at Brighton now known as Roedean. It was founded in 1885, by the Misses Lawrence, with three distinct aims: (1) to give a due importance to physical education and outdoor games in every girl's life; (2) to regulate the school discipline in such a way as to develop trustworthiness and a sense of responsibility in the pupils; (3) to give girls a sound and careful intellectual training. The order in which these are stated indicates the growing importance attached to physical training and public spirit, and explains the lines on which what might be called the reformed boarding-school is proceeding.

This Brighton school is just about to take a fresh departure. It has raised money by shares for a new building on a magnificent site between Brighton and Rottingdean. The new premises consist of a convenient school-house and four separate boarding-houses connected by covered passages with the central building. Something of college methods is to be brought into school by giving each girl a separate bedroom, while the eight seniors in each house are to have a study as well. Here they may give their Saturday tea-parties, entertain their friends, and learn to take the responsibility of their own little domain. The special characteristics of the school are the large amount of responsibility given to the girls and their success in games, of which they are not a little proud. The curriculum resembles that of a high school, with more scope for individual tuition, and most of the teachers are graduates. Wimbledon House School, as it was called before the change in site necessitated a change in name, was one of the pioneers in bringing about the newer view of girls' education. These views are being widely adopted. The increased freedom, the more active life, the great stress laid on the *corpus sanum* as one means of developing the *mens sana*, are all part of the new order of things, and a recognition that the wider life led by the women of to-day needs its own special preparation.

A new school of a similar kind has been started at Aldeburgh, and is being carried on in temporary premises at Southwold on the East Coast. It is proposed to acquire a site here or in some other part of Suffolk, and raise money for building by means of a company. The plan is similar to the Brighton one: a school-house and boarding-houses under the charge of teachers, with plenty of freedom and individual responsibility for the girls. The daily hour and a half of outdoor exercise, the adoption of hand and eye training in the regular curriculum, and the medical inspection of the girls by a lady doctor, are among the more modern methods that distinguish it.

In their fundamental aims there is a close resemblance between these schools. They represent a fresh break with the past. The false ideal of showy accomplishment had already given way to the worthier aim of thoroughness and a more serious mental development. With the intellectual aims came a change too in the moral. The larger life of the day school of itself promoted more freedom and a greater sense of responsibility in the girls, but their moral training was divided between the school and the home, and sometimes suffered from a lack of co-operation between the two. As Mrs. Sidgwick pointed out, when laying the foundation stone of the Roedean buildings:—'Boarding-schools have a wider function, a more responsible task than day-schools. They have to care for pupils in play-hours as well as work-hours; they have, far more than day-schools, to superintend their development in matters moral and physical as well as intellectual.' It is therefore largely in boarding-schools that the newest ideas can be worked out. The worst feature of the old boarding-school was the excessive supervision, and the deceit and silliness it engendered. *Punch's* immortal direction, 'Go and see what Baby's doing, and tell her not to,' might stand as the rule of conduct in many a seminary for young ladies. The atmosphere of suspicion engendered the very faults it was intended to obviate. The giggling boarding-school miss was a type it was not desirable to perpetuate. What was wanted was something that should prepare girls for life and its responsibilities, as boys were prepared at public schools. This term 'a public school' is curiously difficult to define, though we all know pretty well the meaning attached to it in England. It has perhaps been best described as 'one where the government is administered in a greater or less degree by the pupils themselves.' The true 'public spirit' could only develop as the schools became centres of something besides study. With the increase in their sphere of action the high schools have fostered its growth; to bring it to its full perfection must be the task of the modern boarding-school.

Another, and an essentially practical advantage of boarding-schools, is the facilities they offer for differentiation. We are coming to realise that all schools cannot teach all things, unless indeed like Cheltenham, they are really a number of different schools under one head. While many new subjects have been drawn within the sphere of a girl's curriculum, the old still keep their place. The only escape from smatter and overstrain lies in a wise selection, and a girl's general education may gain almost as much by the exclusion of some subjects as by the inclusion of others. With the constant increase of science schools, technical institutes, special endowments for science, etc., selection and differentiation are rapidly increasing in one direction, and it becomes essential to provide elsewhere against the complete neglect of the literary side. This the boarding-school may do without inflicting any injustice, since it does not profess to supply all the local needs. Up to the age of fourteen there can be no thought of specialising; by that time most parents have some general idea about their daughter's probable future and special inclinations. If it is a question of a definite career, the choice becomes easier, because confined within narrower limits.

Yet after all, when we have reviewed in our minds all the careers open to women, and the great social changes due to their entering the lists with trained instead of unskilled labour, the fact still remains that, at any rate in the upper and upper-middle classes, the majority of women do not earn their own living. As Hannah More reminded us long ago, their profession is to be that of 'wives, mothers, and mistresses of households,' and to this we must now add the duties of a philanthropic and public character that social position brings with it. What is commonly called 'a life of leisure' may be an exceedingly busy life, and nowhere do the advantages of mental training, habits of accuracy, and a disciplined will tell to more advantage than in promoting the happiness of others. Most of these girls must receive any education, beyond the early part which a private governess can undertake, in boarding-schools, if only because the leisured classes to which they belong seldom live near enough to towns to make use of day-schools. To quote a very able and experienced schoolmistress:—'The demand for private schools and for the individual attention which girls require has been increased by the habits of modern life among the upper and upper-middle classes. From my own personal knowledge there are many parents who spend nearly the whole year away from home or in entertaining a "house party" when they are at home. There is really no place at home for the poor girls who have not "come out." What the parents seek for them is a school that can supply the place of a home, where they can receive individual attention, cultivation, training, and be prepared for society.' She might have added that, even when there is a place at home for them, they may gain considerably by spending part of two or three years away from it, amid the more studious atmosphere and the numerous interests characteristic of these modern boarding-schools.

The reform in teaching unquestionably began in the public schools, but the best private schools have not been slow to bring themselves into line. Within the last few years several have been either founded or taken over by ladies who have studied at Oxford or Cambridge, or such as have occupied posts as heads or assistants in high schools, and have been drawn into the line of progress, while older institutions have held their own by the introduction of modern methods. Thus, while the old boarding-school was specially condemned for its stuffy rooms, inadequate dormitory accommodation, insufficient food and crocodile form of exercise, the new one, with a rather lower fee, devotes special care to buildings, bedrooms, diet, games, and gymnastics. Here are a few quotations from prospectuses:—'There is a large playground at a short distance from the school, in which are five lawn-tennis courts and space for cricket, hockey, croquet, and other games.' This school has a certificated trained nurse and a sanatorium specially fitted up for illness. The Principal was for many years assistant mistress at a large high school.

'There are gardens with tennis-lawn, a gymnasium, a fives-court, an isolation ward and a playing field at a short distance from the house. Arrangements are made for riding and cycling.' The Principal is a distinguished graduate of one of the women's colleges.

'The buildings have been certified by a sanitary officer, and are fitted with every modern convenience. Arrangements have been made for cricket, tennis, and other healthful games, which are greatly encouraged.'

'The house stands in its own grounds of fourteen acres, which include garden, shrubbery, tennis-courts, and recreation field.'

These are samples taken at random.

Closely connected with regard for healthful conditions is the endeavour to avoid overstrain, and this has led to a not unnatural reaction against the excessive burden of outside examination. We find such sentences as 'particular care is taken to prevent over-pressure.' 'For the younger or weaker of the party we provide extra half hours of rest or recreation in the garden.' 'There is no cramming for examinations, and the object set before each girl is to do her daily work as well as she possibly can from an honourable sense of duty,' etc. It is often stated that pupils can be prepared for university or other examinations if desired, but although some few private schools of this type distinctly aim at the certificate of the Joint Board, the majority work on more general lines, while ensuring a high standard of efficiency by submitting the school annually to inspection by university examiners. The fees in schools of this grade vary from about £90 to £135 per annum, with so-called 'extras.' These are reduced in the more modern institutions to such subjects as piano, violin, and dancing, which require individual instruction, while the more old-fashioned include languages, even French, under this heading. But both terms and curricula in private schools are adapted to special cases, and it is impossible to generalise on them. For girls, as for boys, the statement made by the Secondary Commission is probably correct, that 'the large private schools, usually with boarders, are the private schools which do most for secondary education. They are often conducted on lines similar to those of public schools; but they are less bound by heredity, and the larger scope for experiment which they afford has, there is reason to believe, contributed to noteworthy improvements of methods.'

Probably this class of school is in greater demand than ever before; but though there are not a few who can enjoy its benefits, it must always be a luxury for the rich, while there has been no corresponding improvement in the cheaper type of boarding-school. To provide board, lodging, and tuition, at fees ranging from £30 to £50, is a difficult problem, and can hardly be solved without the infliction of some suffering or injustice. Yet even these fees are beyond the reach of many whose homes are far away from towns. There is urgent need for some scheme of boarding-houses (not self-supporting) in connection with the cheaper endowed schools, and the application of some public money to the establishment of a few large boarding-schools in different parts of the country. Private effort cannot meet these cases.

Private day-schools involve a much smaller risk, and in these large numbers of well-educated women are now at work. In a place too small to support a high school, schools of this kind often supply all needs; but, oddly enough, they seem to flourish best where they exist side by side with good public schools. Bedford is an instance of a town well supplied with both. Sometimes the head-mistress takes a few boarders, and is thus enabled to provide better premises. The fees range from about £12 to £30 per annum, and the curriculum is not unlike that of a high school, though the more expensive subjects, such as certain branches of science, are often omitted. The Junior and Senior Local Examinations and those of the College of Preceptors are a good deal used by these schools, and help to keep up a standard, where a regular external examination is not practicable. Small, cheap day-schools still abound, though happily in nothing like the old numbers. Even these have undergone some improvement, though rumour maintains that *Mangnall's Questions* and *Child's Guide* may still be found here, if we only dig deep enough. The lowest class of private school is attended by children who ought to be in the public elementary schools. The extinction of these, which is rapidly proceeding, can only be hailed with general satisfaction.

Much has been said of late about the necessity of finding a place in any general system of education for private schools, but surely their proper function is so clearly defined that there is no fear of a day dawning when they are no longer needed. A further increase in cheap public day-schools may lessen the numbers, and it is hardly to be expected that in ten years' time the present conditions, under which 70 per cent. of our girls who are receiving secondary education are in private schools, shall still prevail. The true function of the private school is to offer an educational luxury to those who can pay for it, and on these lines, without coming into competition with public school work, it is likely to develop. The more public schools are established in a district, the greater becomes the field for first-grade private schools. This is well illustrated by the case of the United States, where the universal diffusion of the public schools seems to favour the growth of private ones. They can charge high fees, because the public schools are always available for those who cannot afford these. They can try experiments and adopt new methods, because they are not subject to the rigid direction and supervision to which public schools are liable. A great deal of the preparation for college falls to them, and they enjoy a very different reputation and position from the Prussian private schools, which are obliged to adopt the same 'code' as the public. Cheap schools, to be efficient, must receive help with their finances; such help can hardly be given to private schools while they retain the freedom which is one source of their strength. It is probable, therefore, that they will more and more become schools for the well-to-do classes only. There must be some suffering involved in the changes which the near future is likely to bring, even if local educational authorities do all in their power to minimise this, and eventually the lower class of private school will probably go to the wall. But not till the Anglo-Saxon nature has undergone a complete transformation will there cease to be a place in England for private enterprise; and private schools, even though they may be deemed a luxury, will still rank among us as a necessity.

CHAPTER IX

THE TECHNICAL INSTRUCTION ACTS

On June 24, 1890, a curious scene took place in the House of Commons. The Customs and Excise Bill had been dragging its weary way in committee, and making very small progress. The question under debate was the disposal of a residue of £350,000, available from the new duty on beer and spirits. This Mr. Goschen proposed to apply to compensating publicans whose licenses should be refused, but the Government did not care to press the point in face of opposition in the country and small majorities in the House. Mr. Goschen therefore proposed to shelve the matter till the next session, merely 'ear-marking' the money for the purpose indicated. Thereupon Mr. Healy got up on a legal point, and reminded the House that the Budget Bill, which had already become law, expressly stated that the duties in question were to be dealt with in a particular way, and that the proceeds were to be appropriated 'as Parliament may hereafter direct by any Act passed in the present session.' Under these circumstances, he asked, had they power to postpone that appropriation? The Speaker thought they had not, and his ruling prevailed. The result was the acceptance, on August 1, of Mr. Acland's proposal to apply the money in England 'for the purposes of agricultural, commercial, and technical instruction, as defined in Clause 8 of the Technical Instruction Act, 1889,' and in Wales either for technical instruction or for purposes defined by the Welsh Intermediate Education Act.

This sudden turn of affairs took the country by surprise. The county councils, to whom this money was assigned, were now expected to devote to educational purposes the money and energy which were to have gone to the extinction of licenses. From these events date the educational functions of the county councils. It was this 'whisky-money' which gave the impetus to technical education, a term which had been defined by the Act of 1889. Prolonged agitation throughout the country, due to the fear of foreign competition and the rumours of superior education given to the mechanics of other countries, had led to the appointment in 1884 of a Commission to consider the question, and to their report the Technical Instruction Act of 1889, and the amending Act of 1891, were due.

Among the recommendations of the Commissioners were the following:—

1. That steps be taken to accelerate the application of ancient endowments, under amended schemes, to secondary and technical instruction.

2. Provision by the Charity Commissioners for establishing in suitable localities, schools or departments of schools, in which the study of natural science,

drawing, mathematics, and modern languages, should take the place of Latin and Greek.

3. Giving power to local authorities to establish, maintain, or contribute to the establishment of secondary and technical schools and colleges.

Following these lines, the Act defined technical instruction as 'instruction in the principles of Science and Art, applicable to industries, and in the application of special branches of Science and Art to specific industries or employments.' It was not to include teaching the practice of any trade or industry, but it might include any branch of instruction (including modern languages, and commercial and agricultural subjects), which were at any time sanctioned by the Science and Art department of South Kensington. The means of doing all this was a penny rate which local authorities were permitted to raise. Unaided this could not have done much, and very few places took advantage of this power, until the Local Taxation Act of the following year changed the whole aspect of affairs.

The movement in favour of technical education was one that had been slowly gathering force. At first, as so often happens, the blame for the unsatisfactory state of things was laid at the door of the elementary school. It was pointed out that the education given there was not sufficiently practical; drawing was little taught, and that little badly, while science fared even worse. Modelling was almost unknown, manual instruction had scarcely been heard of, 'the pen was the only industrial weapon that boys intended for handicraftsmen were taught to use,' and, except needlework, domestic subjects for girls were terribly neglected. This was true enough, but it was absurd to suppose that a remedy could be found in the schooling given to children under twelve. Such benefit as might be derived from a change in their curriculum was quite inadequate for the end in view. The real need was for a longer school life, with technical training based on a proper foundation of general knowledge. Hence the National Association for the Promotion of Technical Education adopted into its programme: 'the development, organisation, and maintenance of a system of secondary education throughout the country, with a view to placing the higher technical and commercial education in our schools and colleges on a better footing.' It was doubtless for a similar reason that the Act excluded from its benefits scholars receiving instruction in elementary schools.

The money thus provided almost by accident, became a new and valuable source for endowing secondary education; and on all hands claims of the most varied kind were made on it. Administered by bodies of non-experts, who had to learn their business by doing it, much of it was misapplied; mistakes, often of a ludicrous character, were made, and there was some excuse for those producers and consumers of spirits who thought the money would have been better applied in relieving the tax. But in spite of repeated appeals by specially interested persons, Parliament kept firm in the matter; the money must be given to County Councils, and they must learn to use it. How well many of them have learnt can best be realised by a series of visits to the polytechnics of London and the large provincial towns, to the laboratories constructed in public schools, to the ambulatory dairy classes in village schoolrooms, to the beautifully equipped laundries, kitchens, and dressmaking schools all over the country.

Long before these Technical Instruction Acts were passed, isolated action had been taken. The Regent Street Polytechnic, long known as *the* Polytechnic, was already in full work. It originated in a Young Men's Institute, privately founded by Mr. Quentin Hogg, with the large aim of providing a place where a young man could develop all the sides of his nature, and 'find a reasonable outlet for any healthy desire, physical, spiritual, social, or intellectual, which he possesses.' For some years the Institute flourished in Long Acre, and it happened that, just when increased accommodation became necessary, the old Polytechnic, long the home of Pepper's Ghost, the diving-bell, and other joys and terrors of our young days, came into the market. It was at once secured, and the result was an unprecedented rush for membership. Mr. Hogg, who was the life and soul of the Institute, made a point of himself seeing every boy on joining, and on the first night in Regent Street, he began to interview new members at five o'clock. There he was kept at his desk, unable even to get a cup of tea, till a quarter to one in the morning, and by that time a thousand new members had been enrolled. With such encouragement, it was possible to try fresh experiments, and for the first time trade-classes and workshop practice were added to the programme. The Polytechnic thus became a pioneer in technical work. The London Trades Council in 1883 recommended its system of trade teaching to the London trades; members of the Technical Instruction Commission gave it their warm commendation.

Meantime other institutes were growing up. If Mr. Hogg claimed that the Polytechnic began its labours when he took two crossing-sweepers into the Adelphi arches, and made them the nucleus of a ragged school, the People's Palace had an even more romantic origin. It was inspired by the picture, in *All Sorts and Conditions of Men*, of the Palace of Delight, of 'the club of the working-people,' where 'we shall all together continually be thinking how to bring more sunshine into our lives, more change, more variety, more happiness.' Here, even more than at Regent Street, the recreative side was to the fore, and the main feature was the Queen's Hall, in which public entertainments were organised. It had a chequered career, and finally was saved to the East End by the liberality of the Drapers' Company. Since then the educational side has been more fully developed, but apart from the recreative, which is absolutely independent of the East London Technical College. This is an unusual condition, since, as a rule, the Polytechnics, mindful of their double origin, aim at being centres of both work and play. They have a tendency to fall into two classes: those that began as social clubs, and added the classes to their programme, and those that began with classes, and then encouraged the students to form clubs for literary, athletic and recreative purposes.

The greater stress laid on the educational side by the more recent institutions was due to two causes. In 1883 the London Parochial Charities Act gave the Charity Commissioners powers to deal with certain sums, which had been left by benefactors long deceased, for purposes which had actually ceased to exist. It was lucky that this sum of money, which may be capitalised at over three millions, became available for public purposes at the very time when all this stir about technical education was taking place. The Regent Street Institute was chosen as a model. London was mapped out into twelve districts, and a Polytechnic was to be supplied for each, on condition of local aid supplementing certain sums which were offered conditionally. It was not long before this proposal brought munificent private donors into the field. The Marquis of Northampton and Lord Compton gave a site of the value of £30,000, Earl Cadogan gave ground of the value of £10,000; others gave less, according to their means. Eleven of these Polytechnics are already in existence; Paddington alone is waiting for the private benefactors who shall establish the claim to public help. The second impetus came from the Technical Education Board of the London County Council. The metropolis had been slow in following the lead of other counties, and it was not till 1892 that it resolved to apply its share of the whisky money to purposes of technical education. But when it did move it did so in good earnest. The Council conferred full executive power on a Board consisting of twenty of its own members, thirteen representatives of other bodies and two experts, one being a woman, co-opted by the Council itself. The bodies thus represented are: the London School Board, the City and Guilds of London Institute, the London Parochial Charities Foundation, the Headmasters' Association, the National Union of Teachers, and the London Trades Council. Mr. Sidney Webb was elected chairman, Dr. W. Garnett was appointed secretary and organiser, and the superintendence of the domestic economy work was given to Miss Ella Pycroft. The Board has been most successful in its work, and a very complete scheme of technical instruction in London is being gradually evolved. Since the Board's work is educational it is natural that this side has been specially emphasised in those Polytechnics which have been founded since its establishment, *i.e.* those at Battersea, Chelsea, North London and the City.

The help given by the Board to Polytechnics may be thus stated:

1. Equipment grants made from time to time for specific purposes.

2. A fixed contribution of £1000 a year.

3. Three-quarters—not exceeding £500 a year—of the principal's salary.

4. 10 per cent. on the fixed salaries of the teachers.

5. 1d. for each hour's attendance of each student.

6. 15 per cent. on all voluntary subscriptions and donations from private sources.

Provided that the total payment to any Polytechnic under 2, 3, 4, and 5 does not exceed £3000, and under 6 does not exceed £2000.

The Polytechnics are really subsidised from five different sources: private generosity, city companies, ancient and hitherto misapplied charities, part of the proceeds of the 'beer and spirit tax,' grants from the South Kensington Department.

Dreary as are such enumerations of names and figures, there is a special interest attaching to this particular set. The aggrieved ratepayer is apt at times to point to these splendid buildings as an example of the way in which his hard won money is being squandered, quite regardless of the fact that those papers he abhors have never contained any appeal for money for this purpose. London has never levied a technical education rate, thanks to these other sources of income which have given her citizens so much without any sacrifice on their part. The beer and spirit money has acted the part of a fairy godmother to London men and women.

It was made clear from the outset that both sexes were alike to benefit, and thus the Polytechnics have become what our American cousins call 'co-educational.' But the needs of men and women are not always the same, and the special wants of women were considered in the establishment of a domestic economy side, though they are not limited to this. Practically the whole field of education beyond the elementary is open to county council action, provided no aid is given to institutions with a definite religious bias or conducted for private profit. The only subjects distinctly excluded by the Acts are classics and literature. The money is therefore available for purposes of—(1) definite Trade instruction; (2) day and evening classes in Science, both theoretical and applied, and Domestic Economy; (3) secondary education of a modern character.

Under these two last headings great things have been done for girls and women. In spite of the recent introduction into the elementary school code of such subjects as cooking and laundry, it is becoming more and more clear that the brief time allotted to the Standards is not too much for a grounding in general subjects, and that after this should come the preparation of a girl to be useful at home or to earn her living by domestic work. The elementary school girl is too young, the high school girl too busy, to gain much from the wedging of a little domestic teaching into the mass of the ordinary school work. Nor is a cookery or a laundry lesson once a week of much use in giving the necessary skill and practice. Domestic work wants continuous and consecutive practice, for the acquisition of that 'touch' and 'knack' on which so much depends; and the domestic economy schools come in here to supply what is really wanted.

This type of school did not originate in London, though it has taken very firm root there. Some very interesting experiments had been made in other parts of the country, notably Yorkshire, before Battersea, the Borough, and Regent Street Polytechnics in 1894 opened their domestic economy schools, with fifty-four scholars nominated by the Technical Education Board, and the addition of a few paying pupils. This example was soon followed by the other Polytechnics, and the Board now elects 386 scholars annually, who are distributed among nine schools. The course lasts five months, and during this time the scholars receive free tuition, two free meals daily, and the material required for making dresses or other garments. They attend from 9.30 to 12.30 and 2 to 4.30 every day except Saturday. During that time they get a continuous and thorough training in cookery, needlework, dress cutting and making, laundry work and housewifery, with some gymnastics and singing. In addition to these scholarships second courses of five months' instruction, with the opportunity of specialising in one particular branch, are now awarded to eighty-four scholars each half-year. The first course is not meant to train a cook or a dressmaker, but any girl who wishes to qualify herself for such a post gets a capital chance of testing her own abilities and inclination, and there are further opportunities of training open to her, if she desires them, in the second course or at the National Training School of Cookery. Last year four girls were apprenticed in good dressmaking firms on leaving the school.

Mrs. Pillow, lately employed by the Education Department to prepare a special report on the teaching of Domestic Economy, gives an account of the work of these schools. She says: 'Housekeeping and cookery are treated as part of the everyday life of the girls, and not merely as school lessons. The girls cook the meals which they are to eat; they learn to measure and fit themselves for the dresses which they are taught to make, and they are instructed in laundry work in such a way that they can quite well apply their knowledge to the "family wash" in their own homes. The cookery syllabus contains dishes which are well within the reach of the working man earning an average wage; the using up of odds and ends, bones, crusts, and cold vegetables, scraps of meat, etc. receives attention, and the utensils and stoves provided for the girls are similar[17] to those found in the majority of artisans' homes.

'The laundry work is taught on simple and common-sense principles, the only extra aid to speed and efficiency being a wringer and mangle, and, as these are now so frequently found in the homes of the more thrifty housewives, it is well that the girls should be taught to use them properly. The processes of steeping, washing, boiling, rinsing, blueing, wringing, drying, folding, mangling are all thoroughly taught. The washing of flannels and woollens, a part of laundry work which is frequently very badly done by laundry women, receives special attention, and starching and ironing are exceedingly well done by the girls at the conclusion of their course of training.

'The girls are taught the market value of foods. In some of the schools special arrangements are made for this. At Battersea they are taken out to purchase meat, greengrocery, etc. When the girls cannot be taken out to market, they are sometimes allowed to purchase from the teacher in charge of the stores. They are taught to compare prices, to judge of the freshness and quality of commodities, to expend a given sum to the best advantage in the cheapest market, and how to prepare and cook their meals in the shortest time possible.'

The fee for the complete course is £1, 10s., or 7s. 6d. per month, and this includes the cost of all books and materials. The greater part of the pupils come from the elementary schools, but surely they are not the only girls who need such teaching. Many pupils leave the high schools at fourteen or fifteen to live at home in somewhat straitened circumstances. To them such a training as this would indeed be a boon. It would even be worth the sacrifice of the last six months at school, since they must in any case leave without getting the best it can afford, the teaching in the fifth and sixth forms. Girls attending second grade schools, who naturally leave early, would find these domestic economy courses an admirable means of transition between school and home life; while those, whose bent lies in this direction, can go on to the training schools, and either become teachers of these subjects, or earn a living by their practical application. In fact, the domestic economy school is fast helping to raise the home arts into their proper educational place, as affording one among many suitable careers for women, no longer the Cinderella among occupations, who sits among the ashes, because the prince has not yet come to claim her. The neglect of the middle class to use these schools is another instance of their proverbial apathy; meantime, these good things are ready

[17] In character, not of course in size.

for them as soon as they will take the trouble to grasp them. Of course there is no reason why such teaching should be given free, except to a minority.

Even more widespread than these day-schools are the evening classes in the same subjects. These are found throughout the country, in towns at technical institutes, in villages in little classes taught by peripatetic teachers, who are sent from place to place by the county councils. In fact, 'county council dressmaking' has become such a feature, that it might be taken for a special system of cutting and fitting. The persons for whose benefit this instruction is given are young women who have left school, wives, and mothers of families. If experience has taught them their own deficiencies, they have now the opportunity of making up lost ground. Cookery, dressmaking, and nursing often attract large numbers. The teaching has no professional purpose. It is simply 'for home use,' as the Germans say, and has its place in a wide scheme of general education, which includes training the hand as well as the mind.

This village work must, to some extent, be desultory, while, in the large town institutes, it can be made more systematic. Its value is considerably affected by the construction of the board which controls it. A council which places experts on its technical education committee generally does better than one that simply adds education to its other manifold functions. Women are able to sit on these committees, and it is of great importance, for the more feminine side of the work, that they should be appointed in larger numbers than has hitherto been the case.

The female element is represented at some of the institutes by the appointment of a lady-superintendent of the women's department. This is the case in the London Polytechnics, where the women's work is very fully equipped. At Battersea, which may be taken as typical, the subjects taught in this department are: cookery, needlework, dress cutting and making, millinery, fancy needlework and embroidery, laundry work. In most of these subjects pupils can be prepared for the examinations of the City and Guilds of London Institute. The fees are low, and the courses carefully graduated. There is an interesting class in 'homekeeping,' intended for students whose occupation prevents them from getting the necessary knowledge of housekeeping during the day. This includes such items as spring cleaning, ordinary household duties and daily routine, and is probably of special use to that large class of housekeepers who, having learnt their own deficiencies from bitter experience, can value this opportunity of remedying them. Another useful course is elementary political economy, which includes value and distribution of wealth, rent, wages, and other similar problems. This instruction, to which both mistress and maid might listen with profit, can be had by Polytechnic members for 1s., and for 1s. 6d. by outsiders. Members may also join a reading circle and a first-aid class; they can use the beautiful gymnasium, and refresh their cramped limbs with musical drill. All this, with the social advantages which are manifold, is within reach of those girls and women who are lucky enough to live in the neighbourhood of a Polytechnic, and have some free evenings to spend there.

Institutes of this kind are fast being brought within reach of all dwellers in towns. The municipal schools of Manchester and Brighton need hardly shrink from comparison with those of the metropolis. In fact, when we look at the sumptuous equipment of such schools, we are tempted to exclaim that Cinderella has indeed left the ashes, and ascended into her palace. But these glories are not hers by sole right. The men's department (of mechanics, engineering, etc.) is far larger than the women's, and besides these two, where the sexes are of necessity kept apart, there are numerous classes where they meet on common ground. At Battersea the art department is open three days and five evenings a week, and the general scheme includes a thoroughly practical knowledge of designing, drawing, painting, and modelling, especially in its various applications to trades and industries, as well as life classes, and the commoner features of such schools. In the commercial school, arithmetic, book-keeping, typewriting and shorthand are taught, as well as French. There are classes in pure and applied mathematics, and every branch of science is taught with such advantages in the way of laboratories and appliances, as no private or self-supporting institution could attempt to supply. Most Polytechnics are centres for University Extension, some have fine gymnasia, some have swimming-baths; nearly all have a long list of social, athletic, and recreative clubs. In fact, a well-equipped Polytechnic is a kind of popular University, which provides for all the needs of its members, though with some neglect of the literary side. This, too, might be supplied by the omission or insertion of a few words in an Act of Parliament. The Polytechnics and Technical Institutes would thus at once be transformed into the most completely equipped and endowed scheme of secondary and higher education in this country.

With such resources at their disposal, it is natural that Technical Instruction boards and Polytechnic governors should have gone a step further, and tried to utilise their spacious premises and admirable teaching staff for the ordinary purposes of a day-school. Experiments on these lines are being tried in several places. It is thought that by establishing such schools, the polytechnic both gives and receives; if it helps the schools by allowing them to use its premises and staff, it is helped in turn by the training given to a number of boys and girls, who will some day be properly equipped to profit by the more advanced instruction in the evening. The school is largely a feeder for the polytechnic, and will help in time to raise the standard of its work. As such it should be judged rather than as an independent experiment in secondary education.

A joint school for boys and girls need excite no surprise in an institution that started at once as 'co-educational.' But unfortunately, in schemes of this kind there is always a tendency to let the girls come off second-best. This certainly applies to the arrangement of an 'Organised Science School,' which is the scheme usually adopted, both on account of its bias in favour of the scientific side and the power it confers to earn grants from South Kensington. Probably the admission of girls was to some extent an afterthought. The Battersea school had been open over a year before girls were admitted as an experiment. The present numbers are about one hundred and thirty, of whom two-thirds are boys. The average age of the junior division is fourteen, and of the senior fifteen. The fees are £1 a term, including books and stationery. The school hours are 9.30 to 12.30, and 2 to 4.30, five days in the week. The work of the three divisions is arranged thus:

1. Mechanical Division. Mathematics, five hours; Mechanics, three and a half

hours; Physics, three and a half hours; Drawing, four hours; English subjects, four hours; French, two hours; Manual training, four and a half hours; Drill, one hour.

2. Science Division. Mathematics, five hours; Mechanics, two and a half hours; Physics, three and a half hours; Chemistry, four and a half hours; Drawing, three hours; English subjects, four hours; French, two hours; Manual training, two hours; Drill, one hour.

3. Elementary Division. Mathematics, five hours; Physics, three hours; Chemistry, two and a half hours; Drawing, three hours; English subjects, five hours; French, three hours; Art, two hours; Manual training or Domestic Economy, three hours; Drill, one hour.

Its aim is described as the imparting of 'a thoroughly sound secondary education, with special provision for the study of pure and applied science, manual training, workshop practice and domestic economy.' This school is interesting apart from its curriculum, owing to the efforts made by Mr. S. H. Wells, Principal of the Polytechnic, who acts as headmaster, to make it 'secondary' in the full sense, and introduce some of the *esprit de corps* and out-of-school life which are such marked features in boys' 'public' and girls' high schools. The school is divided into forms with a form-master; 'each form meets in its form-room for call-over before school opens for the day, after which they assemble for prayers, which are read by the Principal. These are confined to a few verses of Scripture and the Lord's Prayer; and exemption from attendance is granted when requested by the parent, although only two such requests have been made. In matters of discipline the students have been taught to realise that having ceased to be children they should have given up childish things; they are present to work not to play, and their duty to their parents and themselves calls them to take every advantage of the opportunities afforded; in a word, they are not expected to commit acts against discipline—they are trusted.' Mr. Wells further tells us that 'senior students are told off every day to ascertain the chief events recorded in the newspapers, and to record them on a blackboard, which all the school are expected to read, to be afterwards questioned on the event in their English classes. In the same way a record is made of daily weather observations. All boys are required to wear the school cap, and the habit of "capping" the teachers outside the school is willingly adopted. Each term sees its "drill competitions" between the different forms for a shield presented by the Principal, its inter-form cricket or football matches for a challenge cup presented by the masters, and matches between the masters and school. The end of term sees its gymnastic displays or concerts with acting and recitals, to which parents and friends are invited. Three school captains are elected each term, the method being that they are proposed and seconded, and voted for by the whole school. The captains have authority outside the class-rooms, and their position is readily and loyally acknowledged.' The girls have their games among themselves, though now and then they play a boys' team at hockey. They have their own captain, and are assembled for call-over by a mistress, who has a general control over them, and is always ready to help them with advice and sympathy. Women, of course, give the lessons in cooking, etc., which are the feminine counterpart of manual training; else all the teaching is in the hands of men. The intellectual results appear to be satisfactory, and here, as in other co-educational institutions the girls are quite able to hold their own in class. Of the moral and hygienic results it is far more difficult to judge. Whether girls between fourteen and sixteen would not be better under the care of a woman, whether they do not miss some of that moral influence which can only be exercised by a form-mistress who also takes part in the teaching, are questions that must come up in the near future, should there be any disposition towards co-education in this country. As yet it has generally been adopted rather from motives of economy than on grounds of principle. Institutions like those at Battersea, Chelsea, and Wandsworth are boys' schools to which girls are admitted; although, as a matter of fact, at Chelsea the girls outnumber the boys. The amount of time given to science would never have been allotted had the real needs of girls been considered. It is an interesting experiment, but it will not do much towards solving the problem of Modern Schools for girls.

Even more one-sided in its aims is the type of school which the Surrey County Council is starting. This county is specially deficient in girls' schools of a middle grade, though it contains several good proprietary high schools, and the technical committee is therefore applying some of its funds to the supply of this want. The Wimbledon school is the first attempt of the kind, and must be regarded as still in an experimental stage. Girls who enter are supposed to have attained to the requirements of the Sixth Standard, but in a district where there are no Board schools even this is not always attainable. Hence there are many gaps to fill up, before a proper foundation is laid for the new studies. It is supposed that girls will stay for four years, and should they do so, a most valuable experiment might be made in devising a 'modern' curriculum, essentially adapted for girls. Hitherto in this first year's work the course of study is exceedingly meagre; neither science nor literature is taught; there is a little English history and geography, but the bulk of the time goes to shorthand, book-keeping, commercial arithmetic, cooking, laundry and dressmaking. All excellent things, but surely this is not sufficient intellectual fare for these twelve-year-old children. Another two years at general subjects would help to lay a really good foundation on which the special work could be built up; and it is probable that the shorthand and double entry, and even the puddings and clear-starching, will not suffer in the end for this little delay at the beginning. This kind of work is none the better for being spread out over so many years. It cannot, like the more intellectual subjects, be perpetually presenting fresh developments, which give it the charm of novelty. There seems some danger lest, in trying to elevate the status of the domestic and commercial arts, we should forget that they cannot satisfy all sides of our nature. Girls want something different from the science school, but it must not be a purely utilitarian training. In the true modern school they will learn subjects of daily utility; but just because so much time is given to these, there must be special prominence for all that makes for culture. To the Spencerian dictum that education must prepare for the business of life, we should add Aristotle's wise admonition, that it should teach the right use of leisure. Keeping both these in view we may yet discover the ideal 'Modern School.'

It would not be fair to blame technical education boards because they have not yet solved this difficult problem. Their experience in education is still new, and as far as schools are concerned their best work has been done in subsidising those that already exist. On this large sums are now being spent. To be exact, we may state that during the year 1896–97, sixty-three councils, (forty-two county, and twenty-one county borough) gave direct or indirect assistance to three hundred and twenty-eight secondary schools to the amount of £144,871, 2s. 2d., this sum including the scholarships and exhibitions granted to pupils proceeding to or from secondary schools. How much of this goes to girls does not appear, certainly not half, but at any rate enough to make a very appreciable difference to their education.

Of course, this help is not given unconditionally. It usually implies the representation of the local authority on the governing body of the school, the application of the entire subsidy to purposes of technical education, and observance of the clauses abolishing religious tests. Some counties have special requirements, without which no subsidy can be given. *E.g.* Cheshire demands:

(1) That drawing shall be taught to every pupil except any whose exemption may be approved by the committee. (2) That at least two science subjects shall be taught to all pupils over ten. (3) That one modern language shall be taught, and regular instruction given in some commercial subjects. (4) That each student shall receive instruction for at least three hours a week in mathematics. (5) That the pupils shall be annually examined, and at least twenty-five per cent. of them sit for the examinations of the Science and Art Department, or such other examination as the Technical Instruction Committee may from time to time approve.

Other counties are less rigid in their demands. In London, where endowed schools for girls have been greatly helped with grants, some special condition often accompanies a subsidy. Thus the Owens girls' school at Islington received £300 'to be expended in fitting up the new laboratory and art-room,' the Central Foundation school was charged to spend its grant on fitting up another room for work in practical physics and appointing an assistant science mistress. At the Camden school the board provided an Arts and Crafts room, where cookery and dressmaking are regularly taught; at the James Allen's school, Dulwich, a laboratory has been built, and a subsidy given for an assistant science mistress. Such subsidies, even when given for a specific purpose, help the whole school indirectly, since they set free money from the general funds for the benefit of what cannot be included in that elastic term 'technical education.'

Perhaps the chief benefit yet conferred by county councils on secondary education is the gift of scholarships. It has been left to the technical instruction committees to frame that 'ladder' of which so much is heard on educational platforms. Thanks to a system of graduated scholarships, it is now possible for an intelligent boy or girl to pass from a primary to a secondary school, and thence even to the university. Of course this has been done before now, but never on such a large scale. Since each county is a law unto itself, a girl's chances depend greatly on the place where she happens to live. A girl living in Bedfordshire has no county council scholarships open to her, but the Harpur Trust schools at Bedford receive girls with scholarships from other counties. A Surrey girl has a good chance of winning a scholarship, but, owing to the dearth of girls' public schools in that county, she may not be able to make the best use of it. Happily, there are many parts of England where both schools and scholarships are available, and there will soon be more, if one of the difficulties in the way of the girls' 'ladder' is removed, by the recognition of proprietary high schools as public institutions at which scholarships can be held. This is now being done in some places, to the great advantage of the scholars.

Some counties, *e.g.* Derbyshire, Durham, and Yorkshire, have a very complete system of scholarships, accompanied by maintenance grants, without which they would in many cases be useless. There are few counties that do nothing in this way. The London Technical Education Board regards its scholarship scheme as the basis for nearly all its work. 'The award of junior and intermediate county scholarships necessitates such grants to secondary schools as will enable them to make proper provision for the technical training of the scholars. Similarly, the award of intermediate and senior county scholarships compels the Board to see that the training afforded in institutions for higher education is suitable for scholars of seventeen years of age and upwards.'

The Board gives three classes of scholarships:—(1) Junior county scholarships, intended chiefly for pupils of public elementary schools working in the fifth or higher Standards, tenable for two years and renewable. Of these six hundred are given annually, and fifty are open to candidates from other than elementary schools, whose parents have an income below £150. These scholarships give their holders free education at any approved secondary or upper standard school, with money payments of £8 for the first year, and £12 for the second.

2. Intermediate county scholarships are open to boys and girls under sixteen who come from any school, secondary or upper standard. They give free education to the age of eighteen or nineteen, with money payments rising from £20 to £35 a year. The income limit is £400. They are tenable at public secondary schools and places of higher learning.

3. Senior county scholarships. These are few in number, and intended to provide for specially promising students a training of university rank. They give free education at a college or technical institute, with money grants of £60 a year, and are tenable for three years. Here, too, the income limit is £400.

In 1896–97 London had a thousand junior scholars in fifty secondary, and two hundred and ninety-four in thirty-six upper standard schools. Of this total four hundred and eighty-five are girls. The intermediate scholars, of whom there were a hundred and eighty, were in the following institutions: three university colleges, five technical and science colleges, one training department of a polytechnic, fourteen first-grade public secondary schools, twenty-one second grade public secondary schools. Sixty-two of these scholars were girls. Of the senior scholars only two were women. They pursued their studies at Holloway and the Central Technical Colleges.

All this is, of course, in addition to the special scholarships for Art, Science, Domestic Economy, etc., which come more directly under the heading of 'technical.'

If we turn away from these lists of names and figures to consider how wide a field has been covered by this work in London and the provinces, we cannot but be struck by the developments of these eight years. A system of universities for the people has been started, technical and commercial education have received an enormous impetus, secondary instruction has been brought within reach of large numbers by whom it was hitherto unattainable, numbers of already existing schools have been placed on a firm financial basis, and throughout the special needs of women have been considered. With better building and plumbing, better cooking and washing, we certainly may hope for more creature comforts in the good time coming. But this is a small thing compared with the brightening of homes by the gift of those higher pleasures, without which it has been truly said that life is not truly life at all.

Surely whisky-drinkers need not grudge the extra sixpence which has done all this!

CHAPTER X

STATE AID FOR GIRLS

WHILE private effort in the form of companies, endowments, and individual enterprises was building up a complete, though unorganised, system of girls' education, another system totally unconnected was being gradually developed by aid of the State. For a long time the two were regarded as parallel, with no possible point of contact, except such as might be artificially established by means of scholarships. Now we are beginning to think that we may have mistaken the direction of the lines, and that there are some points of connection between the Board School and the High School pupil.

This change is due to the growing conviction that the education of its citizens is a matter of which a State should take cognisance. Far behind Germany in its adoption of this principle, England did at last wake up to the necessity of educating all her citizens. Whether out of self-defence, to 'educate our masters,' as Mr. Lowe bade us do, or, as Plato would have counselled, to make the men and women of the State as good as possible, the idea of universal education has at last gained a hold in this country. Very slowly, and with immense opposition on the part of the classes who regarded learning as their own peculiar privilege, and were jealous of any intrusion in what they considered their private domain. But they were powerless to hinder; when once the little flame was kindled, no force could avail to extinguish it. From the moment that one generation educated in the new schools took their place as voters, the system was secured. The democracy soon realised that education was a levelling agency, and that it was their interest both to maintain and improve it.

It is difficult for those who are familiar with our elementary education to realise how recent is its establishment in England, and how still more a matter of yesterday the full use of the opportunities offered. England was the last of the great European countries to accept the doctrine of the responsibility of the State for education. Schools for the poorer classes were for a long time either non-existent or a matter of local, largely denominational, effort. The first grant of public money to schools was made in 1832, when, without any previous legislation on the subject, the sum of £20,000 for this purpose appeared in the Estimates. Seven years later this was increased to £30,000, and by an order in Council a special committee of the Privy Council was established, with its own staff of officers to supervise the work. This was the first beginning of the Education Department. Thus gradually, almost imperceptibly, the State was beginning to intervene in education. When in 1858 the Duke of Newcastle's Commission was appointed to inquire into the whole state of popular education, it found that much had already been done, but the great need was for some systematic control. The result of its findings was the celebrated Revised Code of 1861, whose main provisions were:—

'1. That a school must be in approved premises.

'2. That each child must make a certain number of attendances.

'3. That children must pass individual examinations in reading, writing, and arithmetic.'

Thus originated the much praised and much abused system of 'payment by results,' about which so many a contest has waged.

Up to 1870, the whole system had grown up out of administrative machinery, without direct intervention of the legislature. Voluntary effort originated the schools, Treasury grants assisted them. The Education Act of 1870 was intended, to quote the words of its author, Mr. Forster, 'to complete the voluntary system, and to fill up gaps.' Its object was not so much to create schools as School Boards. Where voluntary effort was, by inspection, proved insufficient, a district could be called upon to elect a School Board, with power to raise a rate. A subsequent Act, by establishing school attendance committees for non-School Board districts, completed the system of local control; and the 1880 Act made attendance compulsory on all children up to ten (since altered to eleven), and forbade the employment of any children between ten and thirteen who had not reached a standard to be fixed for each district by its own local authority. Those who could not reach this by fourteen might claim the dunce's privilege.

The School Boards found plenty of work before them. For some years they were chiefly occupied in drawing into the schools the great masses of the entirely uneducated; and the three R's, which was all they could aim at, came to be regarded in many quarters as the ultimate aim of elementary school instruction. But this was a temporary stage, which had to be gone through before the red-brick schoolhouse had become a regular feature of town and village throughout the kingdom. Education was compulsory till the age of ten; children who passed through all the standards would remain at school till about twelve or thirteen. For the masses that might be sufficient; for a select few it was either too little or too much. It served to kindle in their minds a love of knowledge, and to reveal a special inclination for intellectual pursuits, without offering the means of satisfying it. Gradually the need of building a second story on this lower edifice became manifest. A subject much debated during the last few years is the question whether this should be planted on the top of the primary building, or provided by special avenues leading from the elementary schools to existing secondary institutions. But while educationalists were discussing matters in the abstract, the necessities of the case were compelling the existing schools to build their own top story. When the Secondary Education Commission of 1894 came to discuss the best methods of establishing continuation schools, they found that a considerable number were already at work in different parts of the country. The change had come about little by little. Clever children had passed through the standards at an age when it was impossible or inadvisable to set them to work; it was natural that the school should be unwilling to turn them away. Thus originated an ex-sixth standard, and gradually the pressure of the Boards upward brought about the extension of the parliamentary grant to a new standard—the seventh—in which more advanced subjects of study received recognition. Thus while the obligatory subjects still remain reading, writing, and arithmetic, with needlework for the girls and drawing for the boys, the optional and specific subjects—of which, however, no child may take more than a very limited number—now range over several sciences, languages, and mathematics, as well as what are popularly called technical subjects. The great mass of schools are still obliged to confine themselves to elementary work; but with the introduction of other subjects into the code, a new element has entered the schools, and has without doubt 'come to stay.' The next development after the seventh standard was a system of ex-standard classes, which in large schools could be worked without a great addition to the staff. In particular, the instruction of the pupil-teachers introduced some more advanced classes; and as time went on, parents who had themselves enjoyed the benefits of education showed themselves more and more willing to leave their children at school as long as the school was willing to keep them. In this way the ex-seventh standard developed into the Higher Grade Elementary school.

This name belongs properly to two different types of school. The Higher Grade proper begins at the fifth standard, and gives an education for three or four years beyond the seventh. But the term is also applied to a school which includes all the standards, and gives more advanced instruction to a small number of pupils who remain after passing through these. The latter is the kind usually found in London; the former is popular in large manufacturing towns, especially in the north, and it is this which is stepping in to fill an important gap in the secondary system of the country.

These schools mark the existence of a new and vigorous educational impulse arising from below. They are a natural, though apparently unexpected, development of the elementary school, which, according to the words of the Act, is one 'at which elementary education is the principal part of the education there given.' Since the great mass of children do not go beyond the fifth standard, it is convenient in large towns to draw into a single school all who propose to continue their education, and by a systematic course of further study to encourage them to stay on as long as possible. Thus a secondary school has grown up so naturally and quietly on the top of the elementary, that many persons are hardly aware of its existence.

This sudden addition of a four years' advanced course would obviously be impossible without funds, and the Education Department is officially unaware of the existence of any pupils beyond the seventh standard. The good fairy who steps in here is none other than that much abused South Kensington Department of Science and Art. This department, which, justly or unjustly, has come to be regarded as a red-tape-bound machine for examining and conferring grants by a sort of automatic process, has only of late years been brought into connection with day-schools. Though its grants began as early as 1837, their object was chiefly to encourage evening classes, and make cheap instruction possible for those men and women whose occupation or income shut them out from the ordinary means of education. An examination which could be used for the purpose of earning income naturally became popular; and in spite of protests from many quarters, in particular from some artists, who regarded the system of drawing-teaching as mechanical and cramping, there has been little diminution in its popularity as a money-producing agency. The establishment of technical institutes gave it a fresh impulse, since the adoption by these of the South Kensington examinations gave a welcome addition to the institute's funds; and as the money for this purpose is supplied by annual votes in the Estimates, and not by a rate, it provokes none of that opposition which a local rate for any object, no matter how desirable, is sure to encounter.

The connection between South Kensington and the day-schools has grown little by little. The grants were originally meant for evening-schools, but there appeared no reason why day-schools should not also earn it, provided they were willing to send in their pupils for the evening examinations, which for some years were the only ones held. As early as 1872, the department had devised a regular scheme of instruction for schools that systematically followed its courses. Under certain conditions, schools under local management, approved by the department, might be registered as 'Organised Science Schools.' A certain class stamp was given them by requiring that the pupils should as a whole belong to the 'industrial classes,' the £400 income limit being used to define the term. Payments were made for success in examination: for Science, £2 for a pass in an elementary subject; £2, 10s. and £5, respectively, for a second or first-class in an advanced stage; and £4 and £8 for a second and first in honours. Extra grants were made for certain subjects. No payment was made unless at least twenty-eight lessons had been given to the class, or unless at least twenty had been attended by the individual pupil. Payments on similar principles were made for Art. The Organised Science School could also claim an attendance grant, which made it a more profitable undertaking. In return, a school was bound to allot fifteen hours a week to subjects taken under the department. As a matter of fact most schools gave more. There was money in Science, Mathematics and Drawing. Geography, History, Languages and Literature were unremunerative. They must go to the wall.

Such was the course which, originally designed for evening students, was gradually gaining favour in day-schools. A child who passed beyond the standards must still earn money for his school, and this could only be done by means of these South Kensington grants. Hence the wide diffusion of the Organised Science School, in spite of its too early specialisation, and the undue stress laid on grant-earning.

This arrangement marked the triumph of red-tape and apotheosis of the examination system. The narrowness of the curriculum made it unsuitable for many boys, and almost all girls. As attempts were made to adopt it more generally for the sake of the grant, condemnation became frequent. The obligatory fifteen hours' Science were complained of; in 1895 new regulations reduced them to thirteen, and introduced a general *viva voce* inspection, which was to take cognisance of literary subjects as well. Grants are still given only for Science and Art, but the other side is not wholly neglected. Ten hours must nominally be given to literary subjects, though this is held to include manual instruction for boys and cookery or needlework for girls. Less stress is laid on examination. In the elementary course, payments are made wholly on the results of inspection, and in the advanced course partly on inspection and partly on examination. The arrangements are extremely complicated, but they amount to—(1) an attendance grant on all students who have attended a minimum number of times; (2) a variable grant on each student; (3) grants for practical work; (4) payments on examination results in the case of advanced students of Science and Art; (5) payments for manual instruction, cookery, needlework, etc. Such are the means of financing a Science School (the term now adopted), and schools of this description are often found serving the purpose of continuation departments to elementary schools. Since 1897 examinations have also been held in the day-time.

A higher grade school which systematically organises its upper department is divided into upper and lower school, the former under the cognisance of South Kensington, and the latter of the Education Department. A four years' course in the upper school usually leads to matriculation. But although they are in a sense two distinct schools, they fit into each other as the primary and grammar schools do in America. The methods are the same in both, the organisation similar, and children pass from one to the other without that breach of continuity which makes the transition from the elementary to the high school so sudden, and often so unprofitable. It is this continuity which conduces so largely to the success of the higher grade schools, and accounts for the extraordinary rapidity of their growth. As many as seven or eight hundred pupils have been known to enter one of these schools on the opening day; three hundred of these had free places, the rest paid small fees.

There are at present in England 169 Schools of Science, with an attendance of 20,879. What proportion of these are girls it is impossible to ascertain. A large proportion of these science departments are in higher grade schools. Although a higher grade school is not necessarily a science school, while science schools are sometimes found as departments of grammar schools or other institutions, the two are found in such frequent combination that the terms Higher Grade and Science School are not infrequently used as synonymous.

Of these schools the best known is probably the one at Leeds so ably directed by Dr. Forsyth. It is established in a huge block of buildings, and has two divisions—one for boys and one for girls—with a central double staircase opening into long corridors, separated from class-rooms by glass partitions. Its class-rooms are large and airy; it is admirably equipped with apparatus, etc., and has a good playground for the boys, though the girls are restricted to the use of the roof. With its chemical laboratory for 120 students, its physical laboratory, large lecture-room, workshop, gymnasium, etc., its large staff, and 1800 pupils, of whom about half are in or over Standard VII., it testifies with all the eloquence of material fact to the vigorous development of this new educational force. The nature of the work done in these propitious surroundings is best described in the Principal's own words:—'On a basis of elementary education it is intended to superadd a system of higher education which, at a moderate charge, will train pupils for industrial, manufacturing, and professional pursuits. This system of instruction will have its beginnings in the elementary school, but will be practically carried out in a three years' course beyond the standards. It will embrace such courses as:—

1. The Classical (or Professional), in which Latin, Mathematics, Science, and Drawing form the chief subjects.

2. The Modern (or Mercantile), in which French or German, Commercial Geography, Mathematics, Science, and Drawing will receive most attention.

3. The Scientific (or Technical), in which Mathematics, Science, and Drawing form the leading subjects.

A school of this size can, of course, be broken up into a number of separate departments, since these numbers would, in any case, necessitate parallel classes, and the work of the upper school is greatly facilitated by carrying down such subjects as Latin, French, and Elementary Science as low as the fifth standard. This school takes pupils from the second standard. The fee throughout is 9d. a week. It contains a very important Organised Science department, but this only represents part of the work of the school. The curriculum of the girls differs but slightly from that of the boys. They take cookery and similar subjects instead of manual instruction, and calisthenics instead of gymnastics. At one time they were allowed to substitute botany for some of the mathematics, apparently with excellent results.

Similar schools, though not quite so large, are in existence at Manchester, Cardiff, Gateshead, etc.—in fact, almost every large town in England now has, at least, one school of this kind. At Leeds boys and girls are separated in the standards, but work together in the upper school, where the proportion of girls is very small. At Cardiff the two schools are distinct and under different heads, but the highest (matriculation) class is mixed. The plan of putting boys and girls together under the headmaster in the upper school appears to be gaining ground. This seems a mistake, since in schools of this kind the needs of boys and girls are of necessity very different. As far as boys are concerned, the continuation school of the working classes is bound, in fulfilment of its twofold function, 'to carry on education beyond the elementary stage without breach of continuity, and to fit children for their future occupation'; to lay the chief stress on science, mechanical drawing, and similar subjects, which may help the future artisan to take a higher place in his trade. For girls the position is different. In fact, science schools were never meant for them, but they gradually gained admittance for want of a corresponding school of their own. Some persons think it a good course for intending teachers; for the general run of girls it cannot be considered suitable. The most crying need for them just now seems complete separation from the boys' department, and some other scheme than that of science examinations for purposes of financing. A girls' continuation school can hardly be a place for specialising. With due allowance for all possible outlets for feminine energy, it still remains a fact that the great mass of women are likely to lead a more or less domestic life, and the special training for what has been called the trade of 'home-making' does not necessitate a four years' course of arduous study. A girl's future, too, is harder to anticipate. She may marry and keep house, or she may work for her living, or she may do both, either successively or simultaneously. What she needs is good all-round training; if along with this she can get some good practical and theoretical instruction in domestic economy so much the better. But cooking and washing must not absorb as much time as boys give to chemistry and physics, else we run the risk of disgusting our girls for ever with household work. It is absurd to confound a domestic art with a theoretical and practical science, for it can only to a very limited degree replace mental training. This a girl can get from a variety of studies. The more general her curriculum, the better will she be prepared for the very miscellaneous demands of her after life. A certain number will doubtless pass through the intermediate school to the university college, but this may be done without excessive specialisation, and the number who remain long enough to make use of such opportunities is likely to be much smaller in the case of girls than boys. If a fair proportion stay for two years after the seventh standard, we should be well satisfied. If the parents have made sacrifices in order to keep them at school till fifteen, it is time for the majority at any rate to be apprenticed for their future work, or make a place for themselves in their own homes. A girl's preparation for life is not entirely to be sought at school; matriculation is not an end in itself, and a girl who has not sufficient ability to win a scholarship to a secondary school, or a special aptitude for teaching, will do better to turn her attention to more lucrative fields of manual or commercial work. The school that, failing to recognise this, endeavours to drive all its pupils through the same examination mill is neglecting part of its duty, and taking too narrow a view of education. A two years' course is what the majority of girls need to fill the interval between the seventh standard and the age of apprenticeship. If we could give this to all, and something more to the few, the State would not be neglecting its daughters.

Since under present circumstances these schools cannot be worked without some help from South Kensington, various experiments are being tried in organisation, to enable a school to earn some grant and yet pay more regard to the needs of girls than is usually done in higher grade schools. Some adopt the plan of Science Classes instead of Science Schools, registering for examination purposes the classes in science, drawing, etc., without offering up the thirteen obligatory hours on the altar of money earning. Unfortunately this plan is less advantageous from the pecuniary standpoint, and many a schoolmistress will declare with a sigh that there is nothing for it but to resort to the Science School. It is not so good for the girls, but it pays better.

Some day, before too long, a Secondary Education Act may enable us to change all that. Meantime we must give to South Kensington the honour of stepping in when education was languishing for want of funds, and helping us to build the upper story for our board school boys and girls. This department, like the county councils which administer the Technical Instruction Acts, has no power to subsidise subjects outside its own lawful purlieus, nor can it, while we lack a recognised educational authority, award its money grants by other means than inspection and examination. Thus the intermediate school is being forced through the mill of 'payment by results,' from which the elementary school has at last escaped. Perhaps this was a necessary stage for both to pass through; and though some victims fell by the way and there was some injustice done, yet it served to establish the general standard of efficiency which has made the institution of more liberal methods in board schools possible. Similarly the stern South Kensington Department may help to establish a better system of science teaching through its careful inspection and insistence on practical work, and it may certainly claim to have 'succeeded in doing what no other system could have done, carrying science instruction all over the country without ever raising any sectarian difficulty of any kind.'[18] The county councils and the Science and Art Department have become our most important educational authorities, for the very simple reason that they alone have money at their disposal. Both are limited in their operations in a manner that forces them to be unjust to some most important branches of study. Legislation can and must alter this in the immediate future. Meantime the result is to emphasise a class distinction between literary and scientific schools. In making science the distinctive mark of the lower-class school, the Department has brought about the somewhat anomalous result of degrading in the public estimation those very studies which it designed to elevate. An attempt is now being made to improve the prestige of the science school by raising the income limit to £500, in accordance with the new income-tax regulations, and including among schools acknowledged by the Department those 'managed by a public company in the articles of association of which provision is made that no dividend shall be paid exceeding five per cent.' Under this heading come the greater part of our best girls' schools, and this regulation would place it in the power of the governors of these to turn a part of their school into a Science School, or to register separate classes with a view to examination and grant-earning. It would be a convenient way of adding to their income, but whether it is desirable to complicate the harmonious working of a high school by a plan of dual control and a very exacting system of outside inspection and examination seems very doubtful. Should it ever be largely adopted the chief gainers would probably be the private schools, which would alone be left free to take a wide view of the present and future needs of their pupils. There would be a curious irony in such an outcome of all the efforts to improve girls' education by making it a public concern; but as long as there is no compulsion beyond the elementary stage, we may always reckon on a healthy reaction and a revolt against excessive red-tape. Britons never will be slaves, not even to a Department which helps them to educate their children more cheaply.

While the higher grade school is designed to give more advanced instruction to those children from the elementary schools who can afford to postpone their working life till fifteen or later, it has also become necessary to do something for those whose occupations will not allow of continued day-time instruction. The Evening Continuation schools are intended to supply this want. The original night-school of olden time was one where the unlettered rustic or mechanic came to spell out his primer and laboriously manufacture his pot-hooks. Though election statistics show that the absolutely illiterate voter is gradually vanishing from the scenes, his complete extinction cannot be far off, and in catering for after-instruction the amount of schooling represented by three standards may as a rule be assumed. But in early days the school boards had to cater for a very ignorant class

[18] *Report of Royal Commission on Secondary Education*, vol. i. p. 98.

of evening pupils, and the work of the continuation schools was to a great extent parallel with that of the day-schools. For many years the codes insisted that pupils in night-schools earning grants should undergo examinations in the three elementary subjects—reading, writing, arithmetic. As the numbers who passed through the day-schools increased there was a corresponding diminution in evening attendances, and it became clear that the proper use of the evening-school was as a place of more advanced instruction. Accordingly in the 1890 Code the clause, that elementary education should be the principal part of the education there given, was omitted. In 1893 Evening Continuation schools received fresh stimulus and importance from an entirely new Code dealing with them separately. Its declared aim was to give 'freedom to managers in the organisation of their schools' by offering a wide choice of subjects with suggested syllabuses in some subjects. The aims of these schools were now declared to be twofold:—(1) to supply defects in early elementary instruction; (2) to prolong the general education of the scholar, and combine with it some form of interesting employment.

The effect of this new Code was remarkable. The total number of scholars on evening-school registers increased from 115,000 in 1892–1893 to 266,000 in 1893–1894. No less important was the change in the character of the work. To a great extent it has become secondary, although primary instruction is still necessary for many pupils, who are removed early from the day-school and have spent the interval in purely mechanical occupations.

Evening-schools have to contend against several obstacles. Chief among them is the diminished fitness for receiving instruction after the fatigues of the day's work. This seems to vary with different persons, and to be largely a matter of temperament, sometimes of habit. The majority of persons certainly work better in the day-time. Another difficulty is the irregular attendance due to the absence of compulsion and the lack of special inducements. Nothing but the intrinsic attractiveness of the class will induce most pupils to study any other subject than those practical ones, like shorthand, mathematics, etc., which may help them to earn a better living. The framers of the Code, recognising this, suggested the introduction of popular elements in the shape of 'lantern illustrations, music, manual work, discussion of some book which has been read by the class, field naturalist or sketching clubs, gymnastics or other employments of a more or less recreative character.' 'For many of these purposes grants cannot be given, but provided that the managers take care that at least one hour at each meeting is devoted to the teaching of the subjects mentioned in Article 2 of this Code, and that the instruction is systematic and thorough, every arrangement for making the school attractive should be carefully considered.'

The subjects recognised by the Code range from the elementary ones, practically the three R's, over languages and sciences, commercial and miscellaneous subjects, drawing, domestic economy, cookery, laundry work and dairy-work, and needlework. Indeed, it would be hard to find a subject not included, always excepting literature, that step-daughter of English schools. Even this is now being taught under the London Board.

The scientific and technical subjects bring the schools into competition with technical institutes, with the result that in some towns there is an undue rivalry between the various educational agencies. To obviate this, the Science and Art Department has drawn up a new regulation, recognising an organisation for the promotion of secondary education in any county or county borough in England as the local authority for administering the Science and Art grants in its own district. As many towns other than county boroughs have classes working for the grants of the Department, this arrangement is only partially helpful, and there is still much undue rivalry. Where this prevails it usually falls to the lot of the School Board to attract the younger and more casual students, a class that is not altogether welcome at the more serious Institute.

Hitherto the work of the evening-school has been of necessity more or less desultory; and of the two agencies for prolonging the education of our working-class children, the higher grade school seems as yet to answer best. That the other plan has possibilities is proved by the example of Germany and the success of our own Polytechnic classes. A definite place for the evening-school may yet be found in our system. Meantime the school boards hold out the opportunities and invite, though they cannot compel, the multitude to come in. The improvement in the day-school will give a fresh impetus to the evening-school. This much at least it is safe to prophesy.

CHAPTER XI

THE INTERMEDIATE SCHOOLS OF WALES

A land of mountains seems to be a land of ideals. Separated by the elementary forces of nature from many of the currents of life that flow beyond it, thrown on itself, its own resources and its past, it cherishes its individuality with a fervour unknown to the people of a plain. Even ruthless modernity, with its complex train systems and mountain-borings, serves but to invade its privacy, not to change its character. Patriotism is stronger, national feeling more tenacious, the practical side of life has man less firmly in its grip. The Welsh people, with their proud claim to represent the original inhabitants of the island, their long roll of story and legend, their 'estranging' language, incomprehensible a few miles across the border, are still a race apart. Neither Saxon nor Norman, legislation nor intercourse, has ever been able to degrade them into a mere appanage of the English nation.

Among the ideals long cherished here in vain by all classes, was that of a national system of education. It would not be fair to describe the country which produced the sweetest and best-trained singers in the United Kingdom, and could organise and carry out such elaborate musical and artistic competitions as those of the Eisteddfodd, as wholly uneducated, and yet until very recently it was undoubtedly lacking in schools and colleges. Like England, it benefited by the Education Act of 1870, which brought instruction to the children of the wage-earners, but it was the class above these, the professional and commercial, whose means or whose patriotism forbade their sending their sons and daughters to England, that felt the deficiency most keenly. Drawn into the stir, which in England followed on 1870, Wales began to move on her own lines; numerous educational societies were started, conferences held, and every effort made to fan the feeble spark till it should have strength enough to kindle public opinion as well as private enthusiasm. The country was too poor to supply its own needs by voluntary effort. For that very reason it offered a useful field for experiment. Vested interests were not numerous; there were a few grammar schools for boys; but for girls only three endowed schools, and one proprietary, belonging to the Girls' Public Day-School Company. Private schools, mostly inefficient, filled some of the gaps, the rest remained empty.

The last five years have wrought a transformation. Throughout the length and breadth of Wales, whether in large towns or small, there may be seen in a conspicuous spot, looking down on the place from some hill-top hard by, a grey stone building, which a large board informs us is the local County School. The pride with which the inhabitants point it out recalls American enthusiasm; to many it is the chief sight of the place. Here is the goal on which their hopes have been set for years; these school buildings testify to attainment. '*O fortunati quorum jam mœnia surgunt*,' we are tempted to exclaim.

This transformation has been brought about by the Welsh Intermediate Education Act of 1889, itself the outcome of that same departmental committee which recommended the establishment of a Welsh university. Its financial contribution, a half-penny rate, and a Treasury grant of corresponding amount, would in itself have been too meagre to produce much result, but when in the following year the Local Customs and Excise Act was passed, it contained a clause permitting Wales to use its share of the money for purposes of Intermediate as well as Technical instruction. In this way the public resources, *i.e.* the rate, the Treasury grant, and the technical money, could be administered in one fund, and for the general purpose of education, with no express exclusion of literature or culture. The tiresome restrictions, the overlapping of authorities, from which we are still suffering in England, were never to be introduced into Wales; its very poverty proved its salvation; there was a *tabula rasa* on which no characters had been as yet inscribed. Both on account of its own needs, and as an untried field for operation, Wales was chosen as suitable ground for an experiment in secondary education, at the very moment when the institution of a fresh educational authority in England came to complicate existing conditions yet further.

It is an accusation often brought against English education, that we have no system which looks well on paper. This cannot be said of Wales. The system there is perfectly simple. It applies to the whole country, and to girls and boys alike. The money is raised from three sources:—

1. A half-penny rate—the County contribution.

2. A Treasury grant, equal to the amount produced by the rate—the Treasury contribution.

3. The local share of the money from the Customs and Excise Act—the Exchequer contribution.

The educational unit is the county, and the governing body consists partly of members of the county council, representing the separate school districts, partly of members chosen by school boards, university colleges, etc. A very few are co-opted. Each school also has its own body of managers, chosen in somewhat similar fashion from local bodies, while the county council appoints one of the members sent up to it from each district to be its own representative on that particular governing body. The duties of the managers are chiefly confined to carrying out the provisions of schemes, and promoting healthy local interest in the school, for they have little power of initiative, and not always even the choice of a headmaster. All matters of essential importance, *e.g.* whether the schools shall be separate for boys and girls, or mixed, the subjects of instruction, the salary of the headmaster, the limits within which fees may be charged, and the proportion of scholarships to be awarded, are laid down in advance in the county scheme, which can only be altered by appeal to the Charity Commissioners. The action of both county and district bodies is therefore confined within very narrow limits, too narrow, in fact, considering the experimental stage of the schools, and the unwisdom of crystallising initial mistakes into permanent form.

These schemes were drawn up, subject to the approval of the Charity Commissioners, by the Joint Education Committees, which received their authority directly from the Act. They consisted in each case of five persons, three nominees of the county council, and two persons 'well acquainted with the condition of Wales and the wants of the people.' Though the interests of girls as well as boys had to be considered, few if any women seem to have been on these committees, and it is difficult not to connect this omission with the injustice with which they have, in many cases, been treated. This was hardly intentional, but it should have been possible to negative at the outset every proposal for making a girls' school a mere subordinate department of the boys.' These committees were only temporary, to exist until the schemes could be floated, and the control handed over to the county governing bodies. But they led to the formation of a permanent board, not contemplated by the Act. Frequent meetings between groups of these committees, with a view to promoting uniformity of action, led to a series of general conferences at Shrewsbury, which, though not in Wales, is the most conveniently accessible point from north and south. At a series of meetings held here, it was decided to establish a central body, and call upon the Treasury to acknowledge it as the central authority for inspection and examination, and for the payment of the Government grant to the various counties. After the usual negotiations and delays, a scheme establishing the Board was approved by the Charity Commissioners, and became law in 1895. In this informal manner originated what has practically become the secondary education authority for Wales.

The Board consists of eighty members, representative of various local and educational bodies: the Principals of the three Welsh colleges, twenty-one representatives of county councils, twenty-six of county governing bodies, five of headmasters and mistresses of intermediate schools, five of certificated teachers in public elementary schools, three of councils of university colleges, three of the senates, two of Jesus College, Oxford, six of the court of the University of Wales, and six co-optative members, three of whom must be women. The bulk of the work devolves on the executive committee of fifteen.

The establishment of this Central Board marks the completion of the Welsh secondary system. It furnishes a link between all the counties and schools, and exercises over these that general supervision which, in the initial stages, had devolved on the Charity Commissioners. Since the subjects to be taught had been prescribed by the Act generally, and by the schemes specially, the duties of the Central Board were not so much to lay down a scheme of studies, as to see that the course already prescribed was duly followed, that each school was in a state of general and educational efficiency, and that the provisions of the schemes were observed. For these purposes they arranged a system of inspection and examination. The Act had defined intermediate education as 'a course of education which does not consist chiefly of elementary instruction in reading, writing, and arithmetic, but which includes instruction in Latin, Greek, the Welsh and English language and literature, modern languages, mathematics, natural and applied science, or in some of such studies, and generally in the higher branches of knowledge,' and the schemes fixed more precisely which of these were to be in each case compulsory. The Glamorgan scheme, which is in many respects typical, prescribes geography, history, English grammar, composition, and literature, drawing, mathematics, Latin, at least one modern language, natural science, vocal music, drill or other physical exercise, and such other scientific or technical subjects, including shorthand, as the school managers may determine. Scripture is not obligatory, but if included, it must be taught by a member of the staff. Some manual instruction must also be offered the boys, and a little cookery to the girls, but, as is inevitable, where the programme is already overloaded, this side of the work takes a very subordinate place. In all schools Welsh must be taught as an optional subject; in a stated few Greek may be introduced. But even without these additions, the compulsory curriculum is a very heavy one, when it is borne in mind that a large proportion of pupils come from the elementary schools, where the girls, at any rate, have been hitherto confined to reading, writing, arithmetic, and needlework, with possibly a little French and domestic economy. Even English history and geography are unfamiliar ground.

The aim of the Welsh Intermediate, as of the English High Schools, is to give a liberal education cheaply in day-schools; but there is one essential difference between them. While the high school is an organised whole, leading the pupils by gentle gradations from the primary department to the lower school, and thence on to the upper, the intermediate school receives no pupils below the age of ten. Since the majority are between twelve and sixteen, they break up naturally into two classes, according as they have received their preliminary training at a public elementary school or elsewhere. This division is by no means so sharply defined in Wales as in England. Wales is both poor and democratic, and inclines to the doctrine, familiar in the United States, that no stigma should attach to attendance at a school supported out of the rates, since the parents do in fact contribute towards the expenses, though indirectly. Hence we find a mixture of class in both elementary and intermediate schools, which in England would be neither possible nor desirable. The omission of the primary department in the new schools is in fact deliberate. There is already one kind of school assisted out of public funds and accessible to all, and it is therefore not thought necessary to subsidise primary instruction in another set of institutions. The intermediate school is so constituted as to fit straight on to the elementary, and in each school a certain proportion of scholarships must fall to elementary pupils. In accordance with the opinion of many authorities that the transplanting from an elementary to a secondary school, always a difficult process, should not take place too late, the admission age and requirements are put low, and the intermediate school is supposed to branch off from the elementary at about the fifth standard. In Wales, where poverty and dearth of educational opportunities have induced many persons of middle rank to make use of the free public schools, the difference between the two sets of pupils is by no means so strongly marked as it would be in England, but even here schools have two different characters, according as one or the other of these elements predominates. In a district where the population is largely industrial, the lowest possible tuition fee is chosen, and the largest possible amount of scholarships given to elementary pupils. Thus one scheme requires that not less than ten per cent. and not more than thirty per cent. of the pupils in each school, shall hold scholarships, and at least half of the number awarded shall go to pupils from public elementary schools, but there is nothing to prevent the whole number from being so given. In fact, several schools have more scholarships than candidates for them. According, therefore, to the interpretation of the clause adopted, the elementary scholars in a school of a hundred may vary from five—the minimum, to thirty—the maximum. In the latter class of school, the fees are usually low enough to attract paying pupils from the elementary schools; hence these furnish a majority of the pupils, and the school becomes a continuation, often a finishing-school for elementary pupils, many of whom stay one year, sometimes only a term or two, to get what prestige they can from attendance at a school of a higher grade than the one to which they have been accustomed. Those that remain for two years or longer usually do well, if their health is strong enough to bear the severe strain.

The other classification into separate and mixed schools is apt to coincide with this distinction. Of the eighty-four schools now in existence, there are twenty for boys and twenty for girls, while the remaining forty-four are mixed. This wholesale adoption of a principle popular in the United States, but regarded hitherto askance by England, in common with other European countries, is due, as in Scotland, to the force of necessity. It is not as a counsel of perfection, but as a means of economy, that the plan has been adopted in Wales. In a country intersected by mountains, and inadequately supplied with means of locomotion, where distances should, as in Switzerland, be counted by hours and not by miles, access to places that look near enough on the map is often exceedingly difficult; and it is useless to plant a large school-building in a central district in the hope of drawing in pupils from a radius of a few miles. The alternative lay between frequent small day-schools and a liberal sprinkling of boarding-schools. The former carried the day, on the ground that they were more equitable to ratepayers, and more democratic. In almost every county, the committee adopted the more expensive and troublesome plan of establishing and maintaining a large number of small schools, and most of the difficulties with which Welsh intermediate education has to contend are due to that decision. In some places there are schools of forty, or even less, difficult to finance and to organise. These might work for a year or two, but as pupils stayed on and began to range from the Fifth Standard scholar at one end to the Matriculation student at the other, with all the varying intermediate grades, failure became inevitable. One remedy in the case of those small schools which were not rich enough to provide a liberal staff for small classes, was to arrange from the first to mix the boys and girls, thus facilitating the grading by increasing the numbers in each class. In this way better results could be obtained with small means, at any rate as far as class lists and examination statistics were concerned.

Owing to the difficulties of grading, this system is being gradually introduced in many places where it was not originally contemplated; but the typical Welsh school, according to the first plan, was the dual. This was to consist of two distinct schools, one for boys and one for girls, built side by side, in such a way that they might have assembly hall, gymnasium, laboratory, etc., in common, and by the economy thus effected in site, buildings, apparatus, etc., it was hoped that the efficiency of small schools would be maintained. Unfortunately, the advocates of this system went a step further, and arranged to complete their economies by appointing a single head for both schools, to take the superintendence of both boys and girls. Obviously this head must be a man. Though some schemes contain the words 'headmaster or head-mistress,' it is at once explained to feminine applicants that the words are a mere matter of form. Indeed, it would be far better to omit them. The most ardent advocates of women's equality would hardly propose to give a mistress full authority over boys of twelve to seventeen. However excellent feminine influence may be in a boys' school, no one wants to see it supreme there. Though paramount masculine influence in a girls' school is anything but desirable, it seemed the lesser of two evils; and both custom and convenience pointed to the selection of a master. This initial injustice paved the way for many others. Though most schools appoint a senior mistress, who is supposed to have a general control over the girls, it is out of the managers' power, when once they have made the headmaster supreme, to make her position one of any authority. Like all the rest, she is appointed by the headmaster; she has no place in the scheme, nor status in the school, except what may be given her by courtesy. She has no voice in choosing her assistants, nor in making the time-table; her position is often inferior to that of a second mistress in an English high school. This kind of dual school was a new experiment, and it cannot be pronounced a successful one. Where the two departments were kept distinct, except for an occasional interchange of teachers, the real difficulties of classification were not obviated; and one set of managers after another took the final step, availing themselves of the permission accorded in most schemes, to 'make arrangements for boys and girls being taught together in all or any of the classes.' The forms are then mixed throughout, and assigned in turn to men and women teachers. Here the senior mistress loses even her semblance of authority, and the school is under the supreme and undisturbed sway of the headmaster. What number of schools have already taken this final step is nowhere definitely stated, but, as far as can be ascertained, it appears to be a majority. It is in fact the logical outcome of the dual plan, and since the tendency of the change is to diminish the proportion of girls, we may look upon these schools as organised for boys, but admitting girls as well.

The whole question of co-education is so exceedingly difficult that it is unfortunate that Welsh educationalists should have been compelled to add it to the number of complex problems with which they had already to deal. The small schools have necessitated this among other problems. Its warmest advocates do not deny that it makes discipline more difficult: constant supervision becomes necessary; boys and girls have to be kept apart out of class, and an attempt, usually doomed to failure, is made in some schools to control the walk home. The freer intercourse, the element of trust, and the bright out-of-school life, which in England have come to be considered as important a part of a secondary school as the Mathematics or Latin taught there, have little chance of development in the mixed school. That valuable moral impetus given by the direct and constant intercourse between the master and boys, mistress and girls, is missing. Thus they lose what is often the best effect of school life upon our boys and girls: the schools become places of mere instruction, not education; they are but elementary schools with advanced subjects in the curriculum; rivals, and not always successful ones, of the higher grade. Of course this is not solely due to the co-education scheme, but it has tended further to emphasise the social difference between the two classes of schools, and also to put women at a disadvantage in Welsh education, which could hardly have been contemplated by the original promoters. Yet now that this arrangement has been fixed by scheme and made fast by yards of red-tape, it must remain as it is, until some energetic band of reformers shall arise determined to end it. But that cannot be as yet.

The second class, the distinct schools for boys and girls, resemble our English high schools; in fact Swansea, one of the most successful, was actually founded by the Girls' Public Day-School Company, and taken over by the Intermediate Board. The money supplied by the county grant makes up for the diminution of the fees, and the work proceeds with little change. Cardiff is also organised on the lines of a high school, with the chief intellectual work in the morning, considerable attention to games and physical training, and a liberal allowance of teachers. In these separate schools the fees range from about £5 to £9, being slightly lower than those of the corresponding schools in England. The allowance of mistresses to pupils is adequate, the elementary scholars are a small proportion, not enough to set the whole tone of the school. In the mixed or dual school the fees are usually low, sometimes even as little as £2 per annum, scholarships are more numerous, and the sprinkling of scholars from other than elementary schools is very small. Both kinds of schools doubtless have their use, though their aims are very different.

With all these varieties of organisation and character, the schools have a unifying influence in the general control of the Central Board, since all are subject to its examination and inspection. The latter is undertaken by the Chief Inspector, who visits each school in the course of the year, and reports specially on the following heads—

1. Character, suitability, and capacity of school premises.

2. School furniture and apparatus.

3. Facilities for recreation and physical training.

4. The relation between the administration of schools and the schemes under which they are established.

5. The organisation of classes.

6. The school discipline.

7. Courses of instruction.

If a school prove deficient in any of these respects, the managers receive a warning from the Board that future negligence will entail a diminution of the grant. This is a useful check, and a form of payment by result which can only do good, for it counteracts that uneconomical form of economy, which declines to spend on proper building and apparatus and salaries. An element of control which requires more careful exercise is the threat of a diminished grant, should a school fail to do well in the annual examination. This, which is conducted by the Central Board, was in the first place inspectional, and was meant to give the schools the necessary outside impulse. In order to carry out the principle of letting the examination follow the teaching instead of the teaching the examination, each school was invited to send up its own syllabus of work done, but this led to so much needless expense, since there were as many as fifty-three Latin papers set in one year, that some kind of uniformity became indispensable. The present regulations prescribe that only pupils who have been a full year in a school shall be presented for the written examination, and in at least five subjects. Forms which do not take papers are examined orally in one or other of the subjects studied during the school year. The scheme bears some resemblance to the school examinations of the Joint Board, but a new feature is the test in languages of 'ability to read fluently, intelligently, and correctly, passages chosen from prepared and unprepared texts.' The papers set are of varying grades of difficulty, and the schools choose which they will take. Thus in Latin there were seven papers set in 1898, of which the fourth is supposed to be equivalent to the standard of the Welsh Matriculation. Not many pupils are likely to go beyond this, since the schools are distinctly preparatory to the university colleges, which a matriculated pupil can enter. If this standard should in a few years be reached by a fair proportion of pupils in each school, the intermediate system can claim to be successful, for it will be accomplishing its avowed purpose, to carry its pupils from the Fifth Standard to the Constituent College of the University of Wales. For pupils who aim at the Welsh Matriculation these annual tests should be sufficient, but experience shows that there is a tendency to aim at results earlier in the school career; and the chaos of external examinations, from which many English schools are not yet completely emancipated, should be a warning to Wales to be wise in time, and from the beginning concentrate efforts on the same lines. This seems to be best effected by following the example of the Joint Board, and combining school examinations with the awarding of certificates. A scheme on these lines is now in course of preparation, and will probably come into operation in 1899. The subjects of the general examination are to be arranged in groups: *A*. Scripture and English; *B*. Mathematics; *C*. Languages; *D*. Science; *E*. Practical subjects. Within certain limits a choice is allowed from these five groups. Junior and senior certificates are to be awarded on papers of different grades of difficulty. The senior standard is to be carefully approximated to that of Welsh Matriculation, in the hope that the University may be willing to accept it as an equivalent. There should not be much difficulty about this, since the University Court is represented on the Central Board, and the Board in its turn on the Court, so that very close and sympathetic relations are maintained between the two bodies that have charge of the educational interests of the country. The next step would be to win acknowledgment for it as a substitute for the Medical and other preliminaries, and a further stage would be an Honours grade that might replace the higher certificate of the Joint Board as an admission examination to English colleges, and a substitute for the Previous and Responsions. Even this might in time be attained, and the Welsh Board would then have fulfilled its mission of making one school stage lead harmoniously and naturally to the next.

Such is the scheme as it presents itself to the minds of the promoters, who look far away beyond the present troubles of small schools, irregular attendance, and inadequate funds, and see in the distant future the glorious fabric of their dreams: one system of schools for both boys and girls, leading them on step by step till they are ready to enter their own colleges, and thence, if more adventurously inclined, cross the border and ask the hospitality of the ancient English universities. The ladder in its widest acceptation is to be set up in Wales, so close to the home of every boy and girl that none may plead inaccessibility as an excuse for the failure to mount. And this system is to be worked by popular bodies, touching at one end the local schoolboard, at the other the university colleges, so that its foundations may be firm and lasting, 'broad-based upon the people's will.'

Such is the ideal; how far is it reflected by the reality? Of actual results it is too soon to speak, since the oldest school is not yet five years old, and the numbers in them are so small that the whole eighty-four now in existence, including boys and girls, have not together as many pupils as the thirty-four schools of the Girls' Public Day-School Company. There were many difficulties to be met. The ground was new and unbroken, the meaning of secondary education, except in so far as it was expressed by a higher grade school, was hardly understood by the mass of the people. Some schools won a too hasty popularity, owing to the impression that they were 'finishing' institutions for elementary scholars, hence the one-year or one-term pupils of whom so much has been heard. This mistaken notion will be but slowly dispelled, and it is not impossible that in a few years' time, should the Central Board prove successful in its attempts to 'level up,' the number of schools may prove too large for the demand. Many boys and girls who must begin to prepare for their life work at fourteen or fifteen would be better off in a higher grade school than struggling to find their depth in these new waters. The elimination of these would prove no serious loss, and it would clear the ground for a fairer treatment of those pupils, whether from elementary or other schools, who are really able to profit by secondary education. The Welsh system cannot be considered complete while so many of the well-to-do and educated classes hold aloof, helping, it is true, with money and sympathy, but sending their children to be educated across the border. Who shall blame them for not offering up their own boys and girls as *corpora vilia*? Yet, until the schools can offer something to such pupils as well, they must remain one-sided.

Still, with all its flaws, and they are not a few, the system has something to teach England. The love of knowledge, noted even in the days of darkness, the willingness to make sacrifices, evinced by gifts of land and money to new schools, the keen interest in their welfare felt by all grades of the community, and the absence of that class jealousy which tends to check the spread of popular education in England—all these we should do well to note, and copy if we can. Then we may be prepared to thank Wales for teaching us both what to do and what to avoid.

CHAPTER XII

1898

Such is in brief the story of the last half-century, 1848 to 1898. Looking back on what is in the main a line of progress, there seems now and then a check, here and there a retrograde movement under the guise of a new discovery. All this is inevitable, since we are but human. But taking the period as a whole, none can doubt that it marks a very real advance; and this end of a century seems a fitting time to pause and rest on our oars, while we survey the breakers through which we have passed; then once more set forth on our onward path, assured that there can be nothing worse before us than what is already behind.

It is not only for girls' education that the revival has come. A general awakening has passed over the country: men and women, boys and girls, rich and poor, the lady of leisure and the hard-working mechanic, all have had something brought within their reach that formerly belonged only to the few. Three years ago these gains were summarised in convenient form by the Royal Commission on Secondary Education, appointed 'to consider what are the best methods of establishing a well-organised system of secondary education in England, taking into account existing deficiencies, and having regard to such local sources of revenue from endowments or otherwise as are available, or may be made available, for this purpose.' Even now the country is waiting for legislation on the findings of that Commission. When we remember that we have really been waiting ever since 1867, we do not feel over-sanguine of results; but happily events have since then moved in many directions, and the Commission, before proceeding to recommendations for the future, was able to draw up a long list of reforms that had already come about and changed the whole face of education in England in less than thirty years.

First in order of time stands the Endowed Schools Act, which did so much for boys, and rescued something from the spoils for the benefit of girls. Next came the Elementary Education Act, which brought primary instruction within the reach of every boy and girl in the land, and set a new machinery in motion destined to change the whole face of the country. In 1888 the institution of county councils provided that local authority which was to make a system of decentralisation in education possible, while the Technical Instruction Acts of 1889 and 1891 and the Local Customs and Taxation Act of 1890 at once brought these new powers into play, and originated a fresh set of educational institutions in the Polytechnics and other similar colleges. Lastly, the Welsh Intermediate schools, established by the Act of 1889, were providing an object-lesson in the organisation of secondary education.

Besides this public work, the Commission had to take cognisance of the enormous changes in the education of girls, due to the wide diffusion of High Schools and the admission of women to the Universities. 'There has probably been more change in the condition of the secondary education of girls than in any other department of education,'[19] say the Commissioners, and they also note that 'the idea that a girl, like a boy, may be fitted by education to earn a livelihood, or, at any rate, to be a more useful member of society, has become more widely diffused.' Various other changes came under their cognisance: the gradual rise of Higher Grade schools, evolving themselves through inherent necessity with no impulse and little encouragement from without; the many attempts at what has been called Continuative education by means of evening classes; the help afforded to large numbers by University Extension; the improved status of the teachers; the various colleges established for their training, and the many educational societies which have grown into powerful forces during the last twenty years. After taking due note of all this, they declare that the time has come to weld these various organisms into one consistent whole. They anticipate no easy task. 'The ground of secondary education is already almost covered with buildings so substantial that the loss to be incurred in clearing it for the erection of a new and symmetrical pile cannot be contemplated. Yet these existing buildings are so ill-arranged, so ill-connected, and so inconvenient, that some scheme of reconstruction seems unavoidable.'[20]

This touches the key of the situation. The reconstruction must at any rate begin with adaptation, then the gaps may be filled with new and convenient edifices. However much such a plan offends our notions of order and logic, we do well to remember that every one of these structures, jerry-built though they may be, has grown up out of some real need; and before we propose to fit all their tenants into neat little model dwellings, it behoves us to be quite sure that such a plan would be as satisfactory in the working as it looks on paper. The mere fact that of the girls receiving secondary education in England seventy per cent., and of the boys thirty-eight per cent., are in private schools, often in towns where there are grammar and high schools with plenty of empty places, should make the advocates of ruthless innovation pause and stay their hand. The public must in the last resort determine what it wants, and though demand sometimes follows supply, the opposite process is a constant one. However much theorists may inveigh, according to their special prejudices, against higher grade or 'private adventure' or any other kind of school, the fact of their successful existence, even in the face of rivals, shows that they do supply a want; and the only prudent course is to find them a place in our system.

This has been fully recognised by the Commissioners, who wisely suggest proceeding on lines similar to those on which elementary education was at first organised. The local authority proposed in 1867 can now be easily constituted, since we have the county councils to supply a nucleus to which educational experts can be added, as is already done on some technical instruction committees

[19] *Report*, vol. i. p. 75.
[20] *Report*, vol. i. p. 1.

and in the Welsh county governing bodies. The local authority would proceed 'to inquire how far the schools within its area provide secondary instruction adequate in quantity and quality to the needs of each part of that area.' In doing this, regard is to be had to proprietary and private as well as endowed and other public schools, and the report adds the following significant comment: 'We are far from desiring to see secondary education pass wholly under public control, and into the hands of those who are practically public servants, as elementary education has done, and we believe that where proprietary or private schools are found to be doing good work, it would be foolish as well as unfair to try to drive them out of the field.'[21] Where the supply of secondary education is deficient in any part of the area, the local authority should have power to establish new schools.

The functions of these authorities are therefore to fall under four heads—

1. The securing a due provision of secondary instruction.

2. The remodelling, where necessary, and supervision of the working of endowed (other than non-local) schools and other educational endowments.

3. A watchful survey of the field of secondary education, with the object of bringing proprietary and private schools into the general educational system, and of endeavouring to encourage and facilitate, so far as this can be done by stimulus, by persuasion, and by the offer of privileges and advice, any improvements they may be inclined to introduce.

4. The administration of such sums, either arising from rates levied within the area, or paid over from the National Exchequer, as may be at its disposal for the promotion of education.

In this way these local authorities would receive large powers of supervision, but comparatively little coercive control, since 'it is not so much by superseding as by aiding and focussing voluntary effort that real progress may be made.'

The general guidance and direction of secondary education should be committed to a central authority, to include the various departments of Government now concerned with it.

Further recommendations are: the consolidation of existing sources of revenue into one fund; and a generous scheme of scholarships for the poor, in preference to a general lowering of school fees.

These main recommendations, as well as other subordinate ones, seem wise and moderate, fair to all classes, and consistent with their professed aim, 'to draw the outlines of a system which shall combine the maximum of simplicity with the minimum disturbance of existing arrangements.' A bill drawn up on these lines would probably meet with very general acceptation from all classes, except those persons, probably few, who are ready to subordinate the general good to their own private fads. Unfortunately Parliament has hitherto proved unwilling to give time for such a bill. The ill-fated Education Bill of 1896 dealt with secondary education as a sort of accessory to primary; and as, unlike the latter, it has not yet become a subject for party divisions and acrimonious controversy, it is not at present

[21] *Report*, vol. i. p. 274.

sufficiently interesting to the general run of politicians to call forth any special exertions on their part. The private bill brought in last session by Colonel Lockwood expressed the wishes of a large section of the teaching profession. It proposed to form one central educational authority under the Committee of the Privy Council on Education, by consolidating powers relating to secondary education possessed by the Charity Commissioners, the Science and Art Department, and the present Education Department, and to establish local secondary education authorities, to consist partly of members of the county council and partly of other persons with special educational experience. It also proposes registers of efficient schools and of persons qualified to teach in them. The ministerial bill introduced by the Duke of Devonshire into the House of Lords at the fag-end of the session merely proposed to bring together in one office the two departments of Science and Art and Education, under the control of one permanent secretary, and to create a Board of Education on the model of the Board of Trade. To this new department the supervision of endowed schools, under schemes framed by the Charity Commissioners, was to be transferred. The thorny questions of constitution of local authorities, raising of rates, etc., were left untouched. It was not proposed to carry the measure, merely to show the country before the vacation the lines on which the Ministry were inclined to proceed. Thorny as are many of the points under discussion, such as central and local authority, amalgamation of existing departments, etc., they are as nothing to the real difficulties that must follow when these matters of administrative machinery are settled. The inspection and grading of schools, the due consideration that must be shown to secondary education proper and to that part commonly known as technical, the proper respect for existing schools that are good and the ruthless elimination of such as are bad—in these lies the true crux of the situation, and under all circumstances some part of this work will probably fall to the local authorities. An enormous amount of responsibility must devolve on those who first take up the arduous task.

One burning question, which ought to be settled for the whole country alike, is the relation between the grammar and high schools on the one hand, and the elementary schools on the other. Are we to have one upper department for both, or two? Some time ago the consensus of opinion seemed to be in favour of one; that was on the assumption that the proportion of children passing beyond the standards would be a small one. Some such idea seems to have been in the mind of the Duke of Devonshire when he spoke of 'a sound system of secondary schools which will be open alike to the most promising children of the elementary schools and to the middle classes generally.' But this view rests on the assumption that the primary departments of both sets of schools are very similar in their curriculum and methods. This is very far from being the case. 'The elementary schools are not, under the present conditions in England, the common basis of secondary education, nor, though an increasing number of pupils proceed from them to secondary schools, are the public elementary schools the sole, nor, indeed, the chief channels through which pupils proceed in this country to day or boarding-schools of the secondary grades.'[22] The changes that would be necessary in the elementary

[22] Preface to *Return of the Pupils in Public and Private Schools in England, and of the Teaching Staff in such Schools on June* 1, 1897.

schools would be so numerous and far-reaching, and the expense so enormous before they would be able to attract the great mass of the middle classes, that no one could seriously propose to abolish the primary departments in secondary schools, as long as parents are able and willing to pay the school fees. They are a necessity, and would have to be supplied by private adventure, as is done at Cardiff and other large Welsh towns, if a public system declined to acknowledge them. In the interest of what we might call the 'secondary party,' the primary department of the secondary school must be maintained. On the other hand, the teachers in Government schools seem equally unanimous in the view that their own special continuation schools are better suited to the mass of elementary pupils than the grammar or high school. Neither party seems anxious for the fusion, and so long as a liberal scheme of scholarships is maintained, it is possible to do full justice to those elementary scholars who can look forward to a school life sufficiently long to enable them to reach the highest classes of their new school. To allow pupils to enter upon an extensive and liberal curriculum, who are likely to be removed before its real meaning and unity has dawned upon them, is a thing we should never even contemplate, were our notions of curricula and grades of schools a little less hazy than they are at present in England. The board school child, who is sent at the age of thirteen by her proud parents to have a year's finishing at a high school, is typical of the present confusion. There is really no more urgent problem before us than a scientific differentiation of schools.

Still, whatever course legislation may take on this and other problems, whether funds are raised by fresh rate or merely by adding together existing sources of income, no matter what are the constitution and functions of the local authority, this, at least, we may rely on—the interests of girls will not be forgotten. For that we have to thank that little band of men and women who have laboured during this last half century in the face of prejudice, opposition, and indifference to remove the neglect with which England treated one half of her children. This much, at least, is established: no future educational legislation will omit to provide for women and girls. For this we have a pledge in the appointment of women on this last Commission, in their mention in every scheme for a new educational institution that now passes through Parliament, and their recognition on every new elective body constituted.

We have gained, gained immensely. Still, we cannot blind our eyes to some evils the good has brought with it. The very acknowledgment of the right of girls to as good an education as their brothers has in some cases, happily rare, led, under the pretence of equality, to a subordination of the girls' interests. Thus, some of the recent attempts to establish joint schools for both sexes, whether on the grounds of economy or the fanciful plea of imitating the family life in a large school of over a hundred children, does indirectly involve a fresh injustice. What the reformers asked for was a share in educational funds for girls and a better education for the teachers, that they might be qualified to undertake the very highest teaching in girls' schools. The attempts recently made in some schools aided by public money to economise by teaching boys and girls together, abolishing the head-mistress and putting a headmaster over boys and girls alike, while arranging the curriculum and time-table to meet the needs of the boys and letting the girls do the best they can with it, is only a revival, under a new guise, of the old idea, that girls are not entitled to the same consideration as boys. Our modern reformers will not find their occupation gone while they have this old prejudice to combat. It is unjust to the teachers as well as to the taught. Hitherto it has been almost universally acknowledged that teaching was an occupation for which women were by nature specially suited. Is it really proposed to oust them from all but the lowest ranks, and reserve the prizes, the chief inducement to work, for men only? This is what must happen, should there be any wide spread of the mixed schools. With the disappearance of the head-mistress we should lose much of that moral training which has hitherto been regarded in England as no less important than the intellectual and physical. We have hitherto prided ourselves on being in advance of Germany in employing women to teach the highest classes in our girls' schools. Germany is now beginning to follow suit, and by means of special courses at some of the universities and at the Victoria-Lyceum, Berlin, some of the best mistresses are being trained to take these posts. Surely we in England do not intend, without a struggle, to take the retrograde path!

There seems to be another danger imminent, due, perhaps, to the great speed with which events have moved. At any rate, we have landed ourselves in a dilemma. The educational movement has been parallel with many social changes. The fluctuations of business, the lowering of interest, and other complex causes which make saving difficult to men engaged in business or professions, have added greatly to the number of women who must now earn their living. Thirty years ago it was the custom to wait till the father's death closed the parental home, when the daughters, untrained to work, unaccustomed to privation, were sent out into the world, to seek their bread as best they could. So general was this practice even among the more enlightened, that the committee who helped to found Queen's College expressed their belief and hope that 'the ranks of that profession (*i.e.* of a governess) will still be supplied from those whose minds and tempers have been disciplined in the school of adversity, and who are thus best able to form the minds and tempers of others.' We are no longer such stern believers in adversity; we now realise that training and earning cannot begin simultaneously, and, further, we have learnt that neither for Adam nor for Eve should work be accounted a curse. All this has led to a great revolution in thought. Work has been made honourable in the eyes of girls. Already at school they are encouraged to choose a profession and to take the steps that lead to it much as their brothers do. If they marry, the years of regular disciplined work prove a helpful training for their new duties; if they remain single, they keep a purpose and an aim in life. This existence of regular duty, of appointed periods of work and holiday, is the easier life; and now that remunerative employment has come to be regarded as a privilege and not a stigma, the ranks of women workers are fast being overfilled. We have heard much talk of late about *new* careers for women; but the very abundance of the talk serves to betray the poverty of the land. Of new careers there are few. In some cases it only means that the work is transferred from a man to a woman at a lower wage. This is no economic gain to either sex. The field should be open to both alike, but for equal payment. There are also a considerable number of occupations which, if not performed by women, would remain undone, or be done less well. Such are nursing, certain branches of medical work and of factory and sanitary inspection, some kinds of journalism, the teaching of almost all girls and of little boys, to say nothing of the wide field of manual and domestic occupations which fall specially to the woman's share. Large fields of philanthropic and social work are their own special domain, but these are usually unpaid. There is plenty in truth for women to do, but not enough remunerative work 'to go round,' as the saying is. Happily, the working life of many women is short, since marriage or the claims of relations often bring it to a premature close, so that the terrible over-supply has not yet made itself too keenly felt. As yet the sufferers have been chiefly those of the old school who entered the arena unarmed for the fray, and have retired to swell the ranks of the 'necessitous gentlewoman.' But signs are not wanting that even the trained and the capable will soon have to suffer. Worst of all is the pressure in the teaching profession. The delight of the enthusiast and the child-lover, it is also, unfortunately, the refuge of the destitute and the one resource of the unimaginative. The girl who has diligently and successfully pursued her own studies without ever learning to take an initiative or to turn out of an appointed groove can contemplate no other way of spending her life than in passing on to others the knowledge she has herself acquired. If hers is a rich home, salary is no particular object. So she ruthlessly spoils the market for her poorer sisters, and takes the bread from another woman whose very existence depends on her earnings. Meantime the work in the home, among acquaintances, the poor, the friendless, the native town, those endless and varied fields of woman's labour, remains undone. In preaching to our girls the nobility of work, some of us have forgotten to speak of its very highest branches. All honour to those noble women like Miss Clough who never did forget it!

This rush of all women in the same direction, this excessive individualism which has given rise to the cant phrase, 'living one's own life,' is surely a stage through which we have to pass, but which need not remain permanently with us. Much may be done by mistresses at school to revive the dignity of home life, to check the untrue notion in the girls' mind that no work is worthy of the name unless it is paid for in coin of the realm. Unpaid service is the pride of Englishmen; why should it not be honoured by Englishwomen? Still, for most service money is the fitting reward, and some measure of independence belongs by right to every adult, whether man or woman. Why do not more parents try to make life at home a worthy substitute for a professional career? Why not pay the daughter a fair salary for services rendered, that shall make her as independent in the matter of pocket-money and holidays as her college friend who is teaching or writing? Just as important is a certain liberty of action and a little room, no matter how small, where she can see her friends undisturbed and have things her own way. Those persons who are rich enough to leave their daughter a fair income at their death can surely afford to allow her these little indulgences in their lifetime. If she is some day to be thrown on the world penniless or with a mere pittance, then the sooner she sets to work the better. Whenever it is possible, parents should make up their minds, before a girl leaves school, what sum of money can be laid aside for her, either for immediate professional training or with a view to an income in the future. It is reasonable and right that a girl, like a boy, should choose her profession, provided the occupations of home are included among those that are paid and respected. If the growing independence of girls helps to bring about this change, the family too will benefit by this quiet revolution that has taken place in our midst. The *Sturm und Drang* period will pass away, and the time for the quiet harvest must succeed it. Enough, then, has been said by the devil's advocate; it only remains to enter into the fruits of our Nineteenth Century Renaissance.

INDEX

A

Aske's School *50*

B

Bedford College *14, 20, 49, 63, 64*
Bedford High School *46, 66*
Bedford Modern School *48*
Blue-Stocking Club *5*
Boarding-houses *16, 17, 44, 46, 74, 75, 76, 78, 81*
Boarding-schools *4, 5, 36, 48, 49, 50, 73, 78, 79, 80, 81, 110, 118*
Borough *39, 44, 87, 93, 105*

C

Camden School *43, 93*
Careers open to women *79*
Catherine Sinclair *8*
Central Board *108, 112, 113, 114*
Charitable Trusts Acts *41*
Cheltenham *14, 15, 16, 17, 18, 19, 21, 60, 66, 75, 79*
Cheltenham Ladies' College *15, 26, 46*
City of London Girls' School *50*
College Hall *66*
Colonel Lockwood *118*
County Councils *69, 83, 84, 89, 93, 102, 103, 108, 115, 116*
County Governing Bodies *108, 117*

D

Day schools *29, 30, 49, 73*
Domestic economy schools *87*

E

Education Bill of 1896 *117*
Education Company *76, 77*
Education Department *87, 96, 98, 100, 118*

Elementary Education Act *28, 115*
Endowed Schools *27, 39, 40, 41, 43, 45, 48, 49, 50, 73, 81, 106, 115, 118*
Endowed Schools for Girls *45, 93*
Endowments for Girls *27, 39*
English High Schools *29, 109, 112*
Euphues *3*
Evening classes *11, 14, 67, 87, 89, 98, 116*
Evening Continuation schools *103, 104*
Examinations for women *53, 58*
Ex-standard classes *98*

F

F. D. Maurice *11*
Frances Mary Buss *43, 44*

G

Girls' Public Day School Company *28, 29, 31, 33, 34, 37, 49*
Girls' School *25, 33, 46, 47, 48, 93, 108, 111*
Girton College *iv, 53, 54, 55*
Governesses' Benevolent Institution *10*
Grammar Schools *3, 4, 29, 45, 100, 106*

H

Hannah More *6, 7, 79*
Hatcham *50*
Henry Sidgwick *53*
Higher Grade schools *49, 100, 102, 116*
High Schools *12, 26, 29, 30, 31, 32, 35, 36, 37, 38, 74, 79, 80, 88, 91, 92, 94, 116, 118*
Hilda *2*
Holloway College *65*

I

Intermediate Schools *70, 106, 108, 109*

J

James Allen *47, 93*
Joint Education Committees *108*

K

King Edward's Schools *42*
King's College *11, 15, 27, 66*

L

Ladies' Department *66*
Lady Mary Wortley Montagu *6*
Lecture-system *12, 36*
Leeds *24, 67, 100, 101*
Liverpool *24, 28, 67*
Local Customs and Taxation Act *115*
London *1, 5, 11, 13, 14, 15, 16, 17, 18, 20, 24, 25, 26, 27, 28, 33, 37, 41, 43, 44, 48, 49, 50, 62, 63, 64, 65, 66, 67, 72, 84, 85, 86, 87, 89, 93, 94, 95, 98, 104*
Lower Certificate *35*

M

Madame Bodichon *20, 41, 53*
Manchester *20, 24, 28, 31, 44, 47, 66, 89, 101*
Manual training *77, 91*
Maria Edgeworth *7*
Mary Astell *4, 5*
Mary Datchelor School *50*
Miss Beale *v, 15, 16, 17, 21, 24, 26, 60*
Miss Bostock *13, 14, 42*
Miss Buss *14, 15, 16, 21, 24, 26, 42, 43, 74*
Miss Clough *24, 42, 53, 57, 121*
Miss Cobbe *8*
Miss Emily Davies *20, 21, 51*
Miss Welsh *57*
Mistress of Girton *57*
Modern Schools for girls *92*
Mr. Bryce *6, 23, 42*
Mr. Fitch *22, 23, 42*
Mrs. Chapone *6*
Mrs. Makins *5*
Mrs. Montagu *6*
Mrs. Reid *13, 14*
Mrs. Sidgwick *54, 78*
Mrs. William Grey *27, 28*

N

Newnham College *54, 55*
Norman Conquest *2*
North London Collegiate *16, 26, 31, 33, 37, 43*
North of England Council *24, 27, 28, 53*
Nunneries *3*

O

Organised Science Schools *99*
Owens College *44, 66*
Oxford *2, 16, 17, 20, 24, 25, 28, 33, 34, 38, 44, 47, 50, 57, 58, 59, 60, 61, 64, 65, 67, 68, 70, 76, 80, 108*
Oxford and Cambridge Joint Board *25*

P

People's Palace *85*
Pfeiffer Charity *50*
Physical training *22, 37, 40, 73, 77, 112*
Polytechnics *66, 84, 85, 86, 87, 89, 90, 115*
Position of Women *72*
Position of Women at Oxford *58, 62*
Private Schools *26, 29, 42, 50, 73, 79, 80, 81, 82, 103, 106, 116, 117, 118*
Provincial University Colleges *66*
Public School *14, 19, 28, 38, 42, 46, 75, 79, 81*

Q

Queen Elizabeth *3*
Queen's College *10, 11, 12, 14, 42, 120*

R

Reading school *39*
Reformation *3, 15, 39, 50*
Regent Street *53, 85, 87*
Renaissance *1, 3, 122*
Revised Code *97*

S

School Boards *97, 103, 105, 107*
Schoolmistresses' Associations *24, 28*
Schools' Inquiry Commission *6, 25, 26, 41, 42, 45, 47, 50, 52*
Secondary Education Commission *97*
Skinners' School at Stamford Hill *49*
Social Science Congress *41*
Social Science Congress at Glasgow *20*
Social Science Congress at Leeds *27*
South Kensington Department of Science and Art *98*
St. Andrews *46, 75, 77*
St. Hilda's *17, 57, 60*
St. Leonard's School *46, 76*
Stuart court *4*

T

Technical Education Board *63, 86, 87, 94*
Technical Education Boards *92*
Triposes *56*

U

University College *13, 27, 50, 65, 66, 67, 68, 102*
University degrees *54*
University Extension *24, 90, 116*
University of Ireland *72*
University of London *17, 65, 69*
University of Wales *68, 69, 70, 108, 113*

V

Victoria University *66*

W

Welsh Intermediate Education Act *83, 107*
Welsh Intermediate schools *115*
Westfield College *64*
Whisky-money *83*
Winchester College *39*
Women at Cambridge *54*
Women teachers *22, 111*
Wotton *3*

Y

Yorkshire Board of Education *24, 28*
Yorkshire College *67*

9 789361 387234

Printed by Libri Plureos GmbH in Hamburg,
Germany